Early American Andirons
AND OTHER FIREPLACE ACCESSORIES

Early American Andirons

AND OTHER FIREPLACE ACCESSORIES

by

Henry J. Kauffman

Quentin H. Bowers

THOMAS NELSON INC.
NASHVILLE / NEW YORK

Copyright © 1974 by Henry J. Kauffman

All rights reserved under International and Pan-American Conventions. Published in Nashville, Tennessee by Thomas Nelson Inc. and simultaneously in Don Mills, Ontario, by Thomas Nelson and Sons (Canada) Limited.

Manufactured in the United States of America
Library of Congress Cataloging in Publication Data

Kauffman, Henry J
    Early American andirons and other fireplace accessories.

    Bibliography: p.
    1. Andirons—History.   2. Implements, utensils, etc.—United States—History.
3. Metal-workers—United States—History.   4. Fireplaces—United States—History.
I. Bowers, Quentin H., joint author.   II. Title.
TH7427.A5K38   697'.1'028   74–7405
ISBN 0–8407–4323–8

An elegant pair of Federal andirons with fluted shafts, engraved pedestals, and twisted flame finials. Twenty-seven inches tall.

Bowers Collection

Contents

I. COLONIAL FIREPLACE FURNISHINGS *11*
II. ANDIRONS OF THE SEVENTEENTH CENTURY *17*
III. ANDIRONS OF THE EIGHTEENTH CENTURY *33*
IV. ANDIRONS OF THE NINETEENTH CENTURY *61*
V. FENDERS AND GRATES *71*
VI. A GALLERY OF ANDIRONS *90*
VII. MEN OF THE CRAFT *109*
VIII. OTHER FIREPLACE ACCESSORIES *137*
BIBLIOGRAPHY *188*
INDEX *190*

Early American Andirons

AND OTHER FIREPLACE ACCESSORIES

CHAPTER I

Colonial Fireplace Furnishings

A SURVEY of the research done on furnishings of the American home in the seventeenth, eighteenth and nineteenth centuries reveals the fact that a considerable body of knowledge exists about categories such as furniture, ceramics, silver, pewter, glass, copper and brass ware. Scholars working in some of these areas have been very fortunate in their research because some of the artifacts were signed by their makers or were made of materials indigenous to America. Because fireplace furnishings can rarely be identified by such evidence, they have been relegated to unwarranted obscurity. In some cases, fireplace equipment can be identified by markings or by styles which are now regarded as truly American. For example, the so-called "Revere" type andirons with a spiral baluster have come to be regarded as American because few, if any, of this style are known to have been made in Europe. Then, there are also signed andirons which bear the names of identified American brass founders, and there is absolutely no doubt about their fabrication in America. This survey will show that progress along the lines of style and maker identification has been made in recent years.

Another point of interest is the fact that considerable refinement had been achieved in fireplace furnishings by the time the colonies were established. It had been learned long ago that raising wood off the hearth floor increased the draft and caused wood to burn briskly. It is apparent, therefore, that further refinement should be directed toward style and materials of which fireplace furnishings were made. Andirons had little stylistic quality before the Jacobean era, but the progress thereafter kept pace with other furnishings of the American home. In

the Chippendale era, furniture and andirons had ball-and-claw feet, and there was unquestionably a relation between the styles of different objects used in a particular period, regardless of the material of which they were made.

It should also be noted that the scarcity of brass and the relatively easy availability of iron determined that most of the early fireplace furnishings were made of iron, either cast or wrought. Throughout most of the seventeenth century, andirons and other furnishings were made of iron, although some had brass finials, and in at least one rare case, brass andirons appear in an inventory of the period.

The matter of style will be discussed more fully at a later point in this survey; however, it should be noted that the first houses built here, and their contents, met only the minimal needs of the colonists. Houses covered with wattle and daab were not ornamented. The large fire chambers of the fireplaces were not topped with mantel shelves, and mantelpieces did not come into frequent use until the end of the eighteenth century. Most of the colonists came from European homes which were frugally furnished, so there was little precedent for change here.

Because most of the colonists were Englishmen, the absence of surviving seventeenth century American furnishings can be compensated somewhat by examining furnishings found in the Victoria and Albert Museum in London, as well as in museums in outlying districts. Archaeologists have uncovered one andiron and some firetools at the Jamestown, Virginia site, which add a bit of confirmation to those seen in England.

As time went on, the colonists, engaged in agriculture and trade, enjoyed rising affluency in many parts of the country. This economic growth accounts for larger and better houses, more sophisticated fur-

Andirons signed "R. Wittingham, N. York." Signature is on the back side of the pedestal as shown in insert.

Courtesy Kindig Antiques

nishings, and subsequent changes in the furnishings of the fireplace. Before the close of the seventeenth century, citizens of the Boston area were using andirons made of brass; however, only a few of this period seem to have survived.

The early eighteenth century is commonly known as the William and Mary period, although at this early time there was only a little tie-in between the wooden furniture of the parlor and the metal furnishings of the fireplace. Style becomes more evident with the increased use of brass in the Queen Anne period, and by mid-century, the Chippendale style arrived in America from England. Finials on andirons and firetools sometimes matched, and on rare occasions the finials on jamb hooks were included. Columns of andirons were turned with a vase and ring, which was mounted on a short broad pedestal. There were also cabriole legs with ball-and-claw feet.

By the end of the eighteenth century, fireplace openings became much smaller, and, incidentally, more efficient because of the introduction of flaring jambs. Some new double-lemon style of andirons remained tall, but the general trend was toward shorter ones such as the "ball and steeple" style. Strangely, while andirons were becoming shorter, firetools were made longer than before. It should also be noted that in this era, makers in Boston, New York, and at least one in Philadelphia were signing their products. This was fortunate, for the presence of these names has led to an intensive study of the furnishings of that period. And, if there had been any doubt about the American origin of many andirons, the appearance of names dispelled any uncertainty about the matter. The use of fenders was carried over from the eighteenth century into the nineteenth; however, the attractive serpentine shape was dropped for ones which were semicircular or half-rectangular. Fenders of this era often have feet and finials.

After 1820, the style of andirons changed from the short example made by Bailey, Molineux, and Whittingham, to a frivolous array of curves from the top to the bottom of the column. The column was too thick for its height, and it was mounted on slender legs terminating in ball feet. Handles of firetools followed the same pattern as the andirons.

Brass and iron andirons of the seventeenth century. Probably Dutch. Some of this type could have been used in America in the seventeenth century.

Courtesy Kindig Antiques

The slow obsolescence of the fireplace in the Victorian era took its toll on the diminishing number of fireplace furnishings. Coal grates came strongly into fashion, and they required only a shovel to feed coal into the grate and to remove ashes. Some andirons were made of cast iron, with designs which repeated the intricate details of barge boards and porch trellises. Some makers had their names cast on the billet bars, where they were eradicated by the constant heat from the ashes of the hearth.

The need for this survey of fireplace furnishings has been evident for many years. It is not uncommon to find furnishings of the nineteenth century in houses of the eighteenth century, and vice versa. Although the major outcome of the study has been to focus attention on the design and manufacture of fireplace furnishings, the fact has also been simultaneously established that many noteworthy examples were made in America. It is true that some exotic pieces were made in Europe and brought here, but the bulk of those found in the market place in the past fifty years were made here. This circumstance came about because Englishmen were burning sea coal in their grates in the eighteenth century, when Americans were burning wood on their andirons. Happily, in this case, American needs were met by American craftsmen. The high quality of the American product is not unique in American productivity, but it is an outstanding example.

CHAPTER II

Andirons of the Seventeenth Century

A SURVEY of furnishings for the American fireplace might logically be prefaced by some comments about their stage of development at the time of colonization. No reasonably old fireplace furnishings have been found except andirons, so the focus will be on them at the moment. It must be immediately pointed out that a long and colorful evolutionary background cannot be claimed for these objects. Neither the Greeks nor the Romans used them at the height of their cultures. This lack can be partially explained by the fact that these cultures flourished in moderate to warm climates, and the need for them was certainly minimal in comparison to the demand for such facilities in northern Europe.

The oldest andiron known to have survived the ravages of time and many hot fires is an example found at Colchester, England. This Romano-British example is thought to have been made in the third century A.D. Thus, it is evident that the Romans did adapt their way of life to the more rigorous winters they encountered in Britain. This single double-ended example was suited for use on a hearth in the center of a room, and accounts for the reason why only one, instead of two, was needed. Wood was stacked against the billet bar on both sides. It was made of wrought iron, for at that time heat could not be created intense enough to melt the metal completely out of its matrix and turn it into a fluid state for casting.

Wrought iron andirons found at Colchester, England. This is probably the oldest andiron extant.

Courtesy Colchester and Essex Museum

To obtain metal, a hole was dug into the ground and filled with alternate layers of iron ore and fuel. As the fuel burned, a pasty mass of metal called a bloom fell to the bottom of the hole. While hot, this bloom was hammered, and in this way further refined. By repeating this procedure with small partially refined blooms, larger ones could be created until enough reasonably pure metal was available to make the desired object.

The skilled labor required for this operation was at first a rarity, and so only the wealthy could afford andirons. The yeoman probably raised his wood off the hearth by using long narrow stones. In both cases, the smoke left the room through a smoke hole in the roof, located above the hearth.

Possibly the next oldest andiron surviving in the western world can be seen at Pennhurst Place in Kent, England. This example, in an earlier style, is also a double-ended one; however, this one is made of cast iron and is believed to have been made in the sixteenth century. The invention of the blast furnace prior to the date of this andiron explains why this gigantic one could be made of that metal.

The early blast furnace was a large egg-shaped cavity enclosed within walls of fire-resistant stones, into which charges of iron ore, limestone, and charcoal were poured. After about a week of roasting, the iron was separated, and molten iron was tapped at the bottom of the furnace where it flowed into molds or cavities made by patterns of wood in the floor of the casting hearth in front of the furnace. This process greatly increased the production of goods, for after a pattern was made, it could be used an endless number of times, each time re-creating a perfect duplicate. Because cast iron was brittle, the members of the andiron were made heavy so they could not be easily broken. Some examples of cast iron are displayed in the Victoria and Albert Museum, and a lone example was excavated by the archaeologists who worked on the site of Jamestown, Virginia. The billet bar of the Jamestown example appears to be made of cast iron, as do those of the English examples mentioned.

Although the artifacts from the Jamestown site have some evidence of ornamentation, it is minimal and the objects might be described as very functional in nature.

The andiron has a sunken panel on the front of the column and a cherub's head below the panel. It appears to weigh at least fifty pounds and is completely medieval in style.

It is an unfortunate circumstance that this discussion of American andirons must begin on a note of uncertainty; however, the fact remains that there is little information about andirons of the seventeenth century, and obviously, relatively few examples have survived. Some circumstantial evidence does exist to suggest production and use throughout the seventeenth century. There can be little doubt that cast iron examples comparable to those surviving in Britain were cast at the Saugus Iron Works, which started production of iron objects in the 1640's. The need for andirons is very evident, and one might logically conclude that with adequate facilities cast iron ones were made; however, none have survived with proof of production there. As a matter of fact, neither of the two major reconstructed villages of the seventeenth century owns an original andiron of the period. The lack of survivals from the seventeenth century is not a particularly strange situation, for very few artifacts of that era have survived, at least, not in comparison to the survivals from the eighteenth century.

Although there do not seem to be any survivals for proof, one might logically conclude that andirons of wrought iron were used in the seventeenth century, lacking the ornamentation of later examples. These were likely massive as regards to the stock of which they were made. The front column was made of a heavy bar of iron. The bottom end was split and spread into trestle type legs without feet or had low arched legs similar to examples made centuries before. The presence of arched legs on ancient examples makes it evident that trestle feet were a

Cast iron andirons in the medieval style, exhibited at the Victoria and Albert Museum, London.

Cast iron andiron found by archeologists at the site of Jamestown, Virginia.
Courtesy National Park Service

ANDIRONS OF THE SEVENTEENTH CENTURY

Wrought iron andirons with spit hooks mounted on the back side of the column.

Courtesy Schiffer Antiques

regression in style in the seventeenth century. There might have been some type of forged ornamentation on the top end of the column, but in the earliest part of the century, none of brass. The billet bar was straight and turned downward at the back to form a leg.

Certainly most of the andirons of the seventeenth century could be described as kitchen-type, although they were used in a room then called a "Greate Chamber" which today implies a parlor. At a time not precisely known in America, but in the seventeenth century in England, a series of hooks were attached to the column of andirons known as spit hooks. Sometimes they were welded individually to the column, while at other times they were welded together and held to the column with a rivet at the top. Andirons with spit hooks were probably used in the kitchen as long as they were needed there.

Some iron and brass andirons were possibly made here, but were certainly used here. As a matter of fact, it is possible that the work in iron was done here and the brass finials imported. It has been pointed out that the trestle styled foot was a regression, but certainly the brass finials show evidence of advanced sophistication. It should also be emphasized that no large examples with trestle feet are known to have been used, or even existed, at the turn of the eighteenth century. One would naturally expect to find some large examples of this type to have been used in the kitchen, but the early all-iron type with arched legs seems to have been used exclusively. At least, they have survived, and large trestle footed ones have not, if they ever existed.

The mysterious absence of large trestle footed andirons is further complicated by the fact that a smaller variety appears to have been used with the heavy oak Jacobean furniture of the seventeenth century. Most of the types discussed are quite small and light, suggesting use with the delicate Queen Anne furniture of a later period. English authorities on hearth fittings invariably describe them as products of the seventeenth century. It is known that the trestle foot is essentially a product of the seventeenth century; at least, that is when furniture with such feet was used. Data which follows will aid in determining the time of their production and use. As far as the brass finial is concerned, there

Wrought iron andirons with trestle feet and vase and ball heads of brass. These really met little more than the minimum support needed to hold burning logs.

Bowers Collection

is ample evidence of its early use. Alison Kelly states in *The Book of English Fireplaces* that "Andirons with brass knobs on them became commonplace in Elizabethan (1533–1603) inventories."

Other than the use of brass with iron, little comment has been made about the decorative features found on these trestle type andirons. It is known, however, that men have always had an inherent desire for

Cast iron andirons with trestle feet and vase and ball finials of brass. These are more sophisticated than those of wrought iron, but the finials suggest they were contemporary objects.

Bowers Collection

beauty, and there was no exception to this rule in making andirons. An iron ball or scroll could be forged on the top of a wrought iron column, but not on one of cast iron. Therefore, from a technological point of view, he had to add a finial of another metal, or cast finials with the column. Both procedures were followed, and when he added another metal, it was brass. Such a procedure is consistent with the rising technology in the working of brass in England and later in America, and brass made a very pleasing contrast with the gray or black iron.

The use of brass and iron in one object was becoming increasingly popular in the seventeenth century, and the practice continued until the end of the eighteenth century. A cast brass finial was easy to attach to an iron stud formed on the top of an iron column, where it was threaded or riveted in place. Only small quantities of brass were available, for the casting of brass was in a very embryonic stage in the seventeenth century.

To gain a true perspective of the brass technology of the era, one must turn to practices in Europe, for it is doubtful if any brass was produced in America at that time. Most American technology was imported from England, where technology was dependent on the more advanced technology of the Continent, principally that of Germany and Holland.

To probe deeper into the problem, it must be recorded that the manufacture of brass was poorly understood at its best. Today brass is made of copper and zinc; however, in the seventeenth century, it was made of copper and calamine, the latter commodity being the ore of zinc. Thus, refining and alloying the two metals was more cumbersome than if the process would have been based on two pure ingredients. Although England had an abundance of the ingredients, the problem was far from solved at first. An excerpt from the book *The English Brass and Copper Industries to 1800* focuses clearly on the matter:

> But, while the prospects were encouraging (in 1710) one great obstacle was in the way of starting brass manufactories; even at this late date the art of making brass was ill understood, so that

large quantities of foreign brass were still imported, because of its superior quality. The only way to ensure success was to fall back on the old plan of securing foreigners who could teach the English of their art.

Thus, it is evident that America was dependent on England for brass and brass technology, and England was dependent on skill from the Continent to improve her facilities and knowledge for making brass. It is no small wonder that brass was sparingly used in England in the seventeenth century. There obviously were andirons with brass finials, and there is a record of some all brass andirons being used in New England in the seventeenth century, but brass was scarce and expensive at that time.

At the end of the seventeenth century, some far-reaching technological events in England greatly increased the use of brass there, and consequently in America. In the last decade, a rolling mill was operating to produce sheet brass, and a new method of casting brass was evolved. Throughout the sixteenth and seventeenth centuries, brass had been cast into bells and cannon, but there was little knowledge about the casting of small hollow objects, such as candlesticks and finials for andirons. Such objects are best produced by a process known as "flask casting." There is a record of such casting late in the seventeenth century. The situation is described in *The English Brass and Copper Industries to 1800* as follows:

> The two main processes described—battery and wire drawing—were the chief ones employed in the brass works of the sixteenth and seventeenth centuries. By 1700, however, another process—casting—began to replace the old method of battery in the manufacture of small metal objects; and during the eighteenth century it came to play a very large part in the brass industry.

It should be noted in the Shrimpton inventory that the "Brass andirons and Doggs" were used in the Greate Chamber (parlor). Maybe the "Doggs" were of iron? Maybe they served as sleepers.

Courtesy Suffolk County Probate Court, Boston, Mass.

In the Greate Chamber

Item	£	s	d
It: 1: greate Chist, w:th his wearing Apparell Lining & woollen	020	00	00
It: one ffetherbed & Boulster	005	00	00
It: one Red Rugg one Blankitt one pillow	002	10	00
It: one Red Suite Curtains & Vald:	003	00	00
It: one Bedstead & Trindlebed	000	15	00
It: one ffetherbed & 3: old Blankitts 3:10:0	003	10	00
It: one Long table	001	00	00
It: one Carpitt 1: Cupboard Cloth & 3: window Curtains & Chimney Cloth	002	00	00
It: one round table	000	14	00
It: 7: Lether Chaires w:th backs & 4: Lether Stooles & 2: turnd Chaires	003	03	00
It: one Chist of drawers	001	10	00
It: 6: Turkye Quishins	002	00	00
It: 11: Rose quishins	001	16	00
It: 1: Wicker Voyder & Skreene	000	05	00
It: 1: paire of Brass Andirons fire Shoole, Tongs, bellowes & a: paire Doggs	004	00	00
It: one wrought quishin & one gilt	000	05	00
It: 2: parcell of woosters	000	10	00
It: 1: Trunk full of womens wearing apparell	040	00	00

In the Closett over the Entry

Item	£	s	d
It: 1: Lether Chayre 1: Stoole & 2: Joynt Stooles	000	14	00
It: writing bookes & pap:	003	00	00
It: one Bible	000	05	00
It: one Lether hatt Case	000	06	00

£ : 04 : 05 : 00

Although the year 1700 is specifically mentioned here, it is very likely that there was some lag between the practice of the process and reporting it. Thus, one might expect to find some examples of the process before the stated date of 1700.

Before describing the process of flask casting, some comment is necessary to describe the pattern used within the flask. Round patterns were turned on a lathe, of equal halves of wood, temporarily joined together in the middle for turning. When finished on the lathe (slightly oversize because of shrinkage in the casting process), the pieces were separated in the middle and the inner portion scooped out with carving tools, leaving only a thin contoured shell to form the desired object. Such a procedure was common practice for it was economical in the use of expensive brass, lightness being one of the qualities of an early pair of andirons.

The flask was a box made of wood or metal, divided horizontally into two halves, neither half having a top or a bottom, but a sliding device was attached at the ends so that the halves could be assembled and disassembled quickly and accurately. One half of the flask was placed on a board with the hollowed half of the pattern within, the hollow side down. The half flask was filled with sand (pounding kept the sand in place), and turned upward with the pattern on the top. The second half of the flask was then slipped into position over the first, and filled with sand. Ducts were cut into the sand leading to the pattern cavity created by opening the flask and removing the pattern. Molten metal was then poured into the flask, and a perfect replica of the pattern was made in brass. The outer surface of the sand around the pattern was made dry before casting so that the wet sand did not cause the molten brass to solidify before the cavity was filled.

Several half patterns could be placed in each flask with ducts connecting them, and, thus, parts to a number of objects could be made at one time. The halves were joined in the center, and turned smooth and polished on a lathe. This was the traditional method of forming small hollow objects of brass in the seventeenth and eighteenth centuries. The procedure led to a saving of metal (instead of casting objects of solid metal), and to the refinement of designs.

Research for this survey revealed that the technology described above was the common mode of producing small brass objects in the seventeenth century, and it seemed perfectly suited for the production of the few brass andiron parts which have survived from the latest part of the century. However, when all the t's were crossed and i's dotted, an inventory of Henry Shrimpton (who died in Boston in 1666) was found, and in it seventeen pairs of brass andirons are listed. To say the least, this discovery "upset the applecart." Many questions remain unanswered. Were they totally made of brass, or did they have iron legs? Were the legs bowed or the trestle type? Were the brass parts hollow or solid? How big were they? Did they resemble the few surviving specimens of the seventeenth century? These questions will probably never be answered, but it is known now that brass andirons were made and used in the seventeenth century.

Andirons of paktong with square pedestals and square tapering shafts. Late eighteenth century. Probably English.

Courtesy Henry Francis DuPont Winterthur Museum

CHAPTER III

Andirons of the Eighteenth Century

BEFORE exploring in detail the many facets of andirons of the eighteenth century, we should look at such broad matters as style, materials, modes of construction, etc. For example, all changes did not occur at the turn of the century, or at any other precise division of time. Elements of one style linger, while new ones are created, and the two are used together for a considerable length of time. The selection of the turn of the eighteenth century as a dividing point is merely an author's prerogative, a procedure which is followed for purposes of organization.

In discussing the style of andirons, one must realize that the notion that andirons have a style will be a new and novel concept to many. It is a common assumption that andirons are a contrivance for lifting wood off the hearth to increase the draft and promote better burning. There is little awareness that andirons, like other articles of furniture, might fall into categories such as Queen Anne and Chippendale. As a matter of fact, it is almost necessary to further characterize such periods as "early" and "late."

In addition to style, another facet of information about andirons is the material of which they were made. To mention brass and iron would certainly cover all the materials of at least ninety percent of the andirons; the only other metal used in an appreciable amount was bronze. The use of bronze might be attributed to the fact that all brass founders were looking for scrap metal in the eighteenth century, and they used what they could acquire, be it either brass or bronze. Bronze was used widely for cannons and church bells, and it is likely that such scrap came to the founders, and they used it.

At least one pair of andirons is known to have been made of paktong (copper and nickel alloy), although the style of these andirons suggests production in Britain. The billet bars and the stems through most hollow andirons were usually made of wrought iron; however, the billet bars of cast iron andirons were usually made of cast iron.

The mode of manufacturing most brass and bronze andirons was by hollow casting and assembling the parts, but on a much larger scale than in making the brass heads for the early andirons. Most of the iron parts are forged, except the various parts of a cast iron one. It should also be noted that andirons of cast iron were made from the very start to the Victorian era. Of course, they differed greatly in style from those made of brass or bronze. It should be noted also that although both metals were cast, the patterns were not interchangeably used. It would be a very curious situation to see the same pattern in both brass and iron.

Now we go back to the beginning of the eighteenth century to pick up the story of andirons when they were made of two pieces of iron and trestle feet, with or without a brass head. There were two major changes in these simple objects; one was concerned with the trestle foot, the other with the vertical column.

The trestle foot might be described as, at best, an expedient. The split ends of the bar were bent outward to set flat on the hearth. If the hearth was uneven, or the foot lodged on a stone or stick, the andiron would not stand straight. To prevent this condition, the area of contact with the hearth was reduced by raising the center portion of the foot, thus creating a flat, low arch with a foot at each end. This foot resembled a large penny, and therefore, was called a penny foot.

By raising the foot off the floor a bit, more elegance was given to the formerly very simple andiron, and further change was effected in the column. A flat lower part was continued on which was mounted a baluster shaft, topped by a larger brass head than had been formerly

Andirons of iron and brass showing the first transitional change from the earlier examples with a trestle foot toward a more sophisticated style which appeared later in the century. Ca. 1720.

Courtesy Colonial Williamsburg

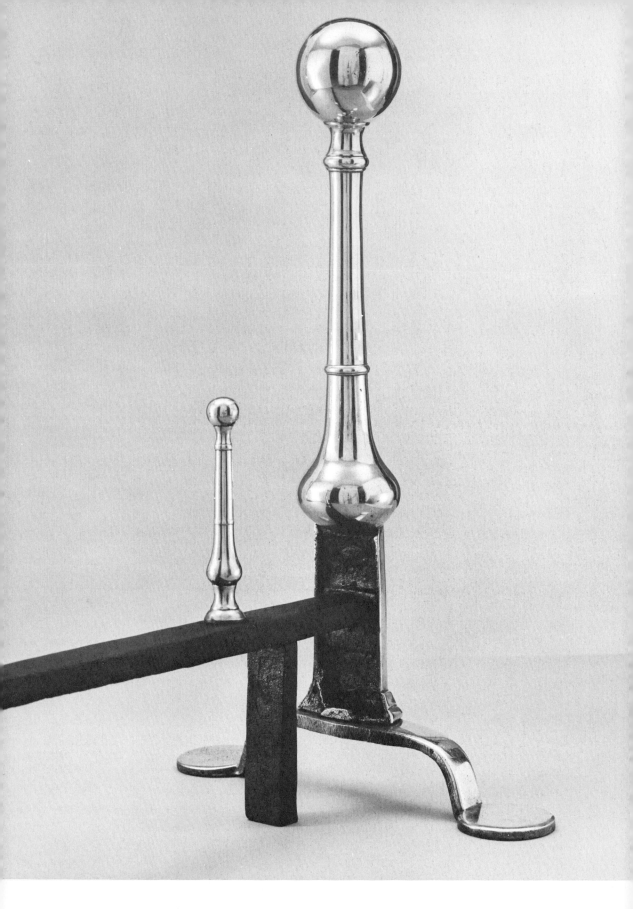

ANDIRONS OF THE EIGHTEENTH CENTURY

used. The larger (longer) brass head was a step toward an all-brass column. The baluster shape was doubtless borrowed from an earlier use in architecture, and it is very evident that a more sophisticated design for andirons was on its way.

At this time, there were two additions to the andiron: a log stop mounted on top of the billet bar, and a vertical support underneath it to keep the bar from bending downward when it became very hot. These latter additions continued to be important parts of andirons throughout the eighteenth and early nineteenth centuries.

The next step was to more or less retain the form of the all-iron andiron, and to make the parts of brass, excluding the billet bar. The flat portion just above the legs had narrow sides which formed it into a channel shape. The back side was open so the billet bar could be continued to be attached in the earlier manner. The baluster shaft was continued, but now made completely of brass with a ball form on each end. The earlier low bowed legs were continued. They were also made of brass.

Brass andiron with low-arched legs, billet bar support, and log stop. The detailed photograph shows the billet bar and the legs were fastened to the column with rivets. The two sections of the column were brazed together.
Courtesy Colonial Williamsburg

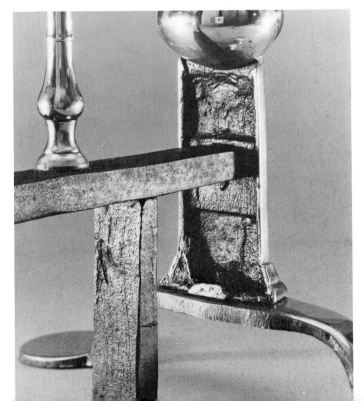

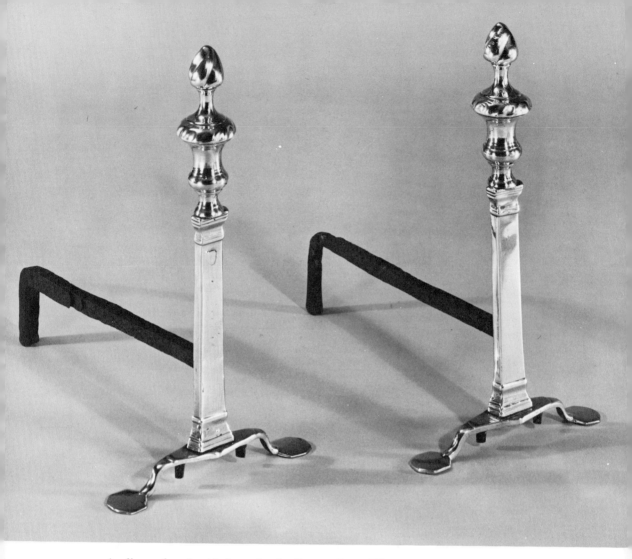

Andirons faced with brass in the James Getty House in Williamsburg.
Courtesy Colonial Williamsburg

Another interesting example of an all-brass andiron with low bowed legs is a pair with a shaft of iron enclosed in a thin case of brass. This treatment was an obvious attempt to have a full shaft of brass with an economical use of the reasonably scarce and expensive metal. Further economy was achieved by covering only three sides of the column, the back side not being seen when the andirons stood in a fireplace. Only one pair of this type is known to the writers, and it is in the James Getty House in Colonial Williamsburg, Virginia. This is a perfect

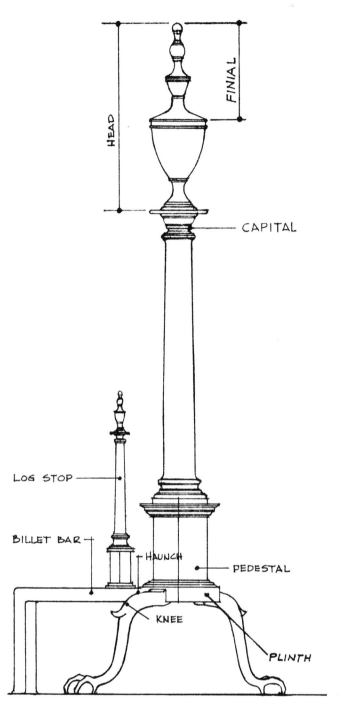

Drawing of a classical andiron with terms identifying the various parts.

setting for the andirons for in the 1744 inventory of James Getty is listed "I pr Iron Dogs faced with Brass 30/."

Although there is little evidence in the Getty andirons, the front columns of andirons were slowly assuming the shape of an ancient column in architecture. The bottom of the column was a molding called

Brass andirons in the style of Queen Anne with pad feet, a short round pedestal, turned column, and a head comprised of a compressed ball and a twisted flame finial. The cabriole legs have molded ends next to the column, two spurs on each leg, and pad feet.

Courtesy David Stockwell

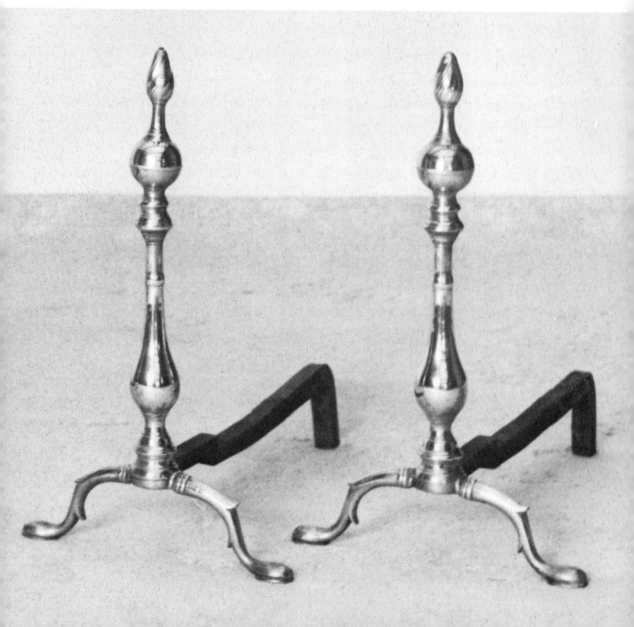

Brass and cast iron andirons in the Queen Anne style. These have the unusual height of twenty-five inches. Similar examples are known which have a diamond and flame head.

Bowers Collection

the plinth, above which was a round or flat area called the pedestal. Above the pedestal was the shaft, which was topped with a molding comparable to the capital of a column. Finally, at the very top was a head which usually terminated in a small finial.

The next style in the evolving pattern of andirons is known as Queen Anne, 1725–1760. The column was dominated by two bulbous forms, one at the bottom, the other at the top, or the head. The head usually was composed of a compressed ball with a twisted flame finial. A new form was also evident in the new S-curve of the cabriole legs, which terminated in a pad or ball-and-claw foot. From a functional point of view, the round cross section of the high-arched legs with a greater spread was stronger than the earlier flat low-arched legs. The whole assemblage was raised higher above the hearth floor resulting in a better draft for the fire and a very pleasing arrangement of the various components. To relieve the longer span of the newly elongated legs, spurs were added above and below the knees. These spurs were increased in size and continued on later styles of andirons. The style of these andirons was in harmony with the furniture of the period.

At mid-century, other reasonably sophisticated andirons were made of iron with a brass finial. Some were wrought and some were cast. The legs are round in cross section like the contemporary ones of brass, but the ball-like design on the bottom of the column is more pronounced. As the shaft rises toward the head, the diameter increases until it reaches the bottom edge, where a series of ridges or moldings brings the diameter of the shaft to meet the base of the head. There is considerable variation in the shapes of the heads, as well as other variations. Many have log stops but few have supports for the billet bars. One might imagine that supports for billet bars were not needed, but this is not the case. The billet bars on andirons lacking the support are often bent downward under the weight of the logs and the softening heat of the fire.

A newspaper advertisement by Mary Jackson of Boston, and the scarcity of English counterparts, are the major evidences supporting

American production of andirons in the Queen Anne period. The Mary Jackson advertisement follows:

> Braziers' Wares.—Mary Jackson, at the Brazen-Head, in Cornhill, makes and sells all sorts of Brass and Founders Ware, as Hearths, Fenders, Shovels and Tongs, Hand-Irons (andirons) Candlesticks, Brasses for Chaises and Saddles, of the newest fashion; all sorts of Mill Brasses; Mortars, Crocks, large and small, all sorts of polish'd Brazier's Ware, at reasonable Rates. A quantity of large Brown Paper for Sheathing ships, to be sold: Likewise buys old Copper, Brass, Pewter, Lead and Iron. *Boston Gazette*, Sept. 27/Oct. 4, 1736

In discussing the andirons of any period, it is necessary for the observer to keep one eye on the andirons and the other on the houses in which they were used. It is apparent that the early examples of iron were well suited to the medieval type houses in which they were used in the seventeenth century. The rising tide of prosperity in the early part of the eighteenth century brought houses which were larger, more agreeably furnished, and more appropriate as settings for andirons of iron and brass and all-brass which were used in them. By looking ahead from the vantage point of mid-century, one could foresee that the andirons of the past would be inadequate, and that more fastidious examples would be needed to fit the decor of these houses. Along the Atlantic seaboard, fine homes were built such as the Dey Mansion (1740) in New Jersey, Van Cortlandt Manor (1748) in New York, Kenmore (1752) in Virginia, Woodford (1742–1756) in Pennsylvania, and the Lee Mansion (1768) in Massachusetts. Of course, many less pretentious houses were built in all of the areas mentioned, the owners of which would be looking for the newest fashion in andirons. An examination of these houses quickly reveals that American craftsmen had to supply furnishings for them. There was not only the fact of rising indigenous fashions in America, but also, that Englishmen were burning coal in their grates at this time. Thus, grates had a high priority in England, and andirons in America. The result was that the lack of supply from England forced brass founders here into creating some reasonably unique andirons for American fireplaces.

The pulse of the times can possibly best be felt by examining a 1770 receipt for andirons made by the famous Philadelphia brass founder Daniel King, and sold to John Cadwalater, of the same city. Among six pairs of andirons listed on the receipt is an entry "to one Pare of Best Rate Fier Dogs with Corinthen Coloms, £25/." This price is amazing when it is considered that Cadwalater paid Thomas Affleck only £10 each for his mahogany desk and great sofa. King's April 20, 1767, advertisement in the *Pennsylvania Gazette* points out that he had "a new and Curious set of Patterns for Brass Fire Dogs, neater and more to Order than any yet made on the continent." This advertisement contains information about the business of brass founding. For example, it is virtually the only statement of the fact that patterns were needed for making andirons. It might also be parenthetically noted that the printer did not use the phonetic spelling which King used in his receipt. It might be surmised that he had little formal schooling along academic lines, but there is evidence that he was a skilled craftsman.

A further word of explanation might also be made about the "Corinthen Coloms" appearing as a style in America. There might appear to be some incongruity in the matter, but the background is well known, for it goes back to Europe, as many similar matters did at that time. At mid-century, excavations were made at the buried cities of Herculaneum and Pompeii. Robert and William Adam, famous English architects, were so intrigued by the charm and beauty of architectural finds uncovered there that they incorporated many of their features into architectural plans at home. This style, like the designs

King/Cadwalater invoice listing objects Cadwalater bought from King including "Corinthen Colom" andirons, "Dovetale Hinges" and numerous other items. The "Roting Stone" was used to polish andirons and other objects of brass.

Courtesy Historical Society of Pennsylvania

1770 John Cadwalader Esqr to Danl King   Dr

Sepr 4th: to a Large Brass knocker of the New Consruction — 1:14:0
to a Scugin & Drop for the frunt Door 3/6 — 0:3:6
to 8 Dove tale hinges at 25/ Each — 10:0:0
to 4 hinges for Blank Doors at 15/ Each — 3:0:0
to 2 Scugings & Drops for the Blank Door — 0:7:6
to one Pare of the Best Rote fier Dogs
   With Crinthen Coloms £25 — 25:0:0
to a Pare of the Best fluted Do With
   Cunter fluts £10 — 10:0:0
to one Pare Do Plane fluted Do — 9:0:0
to one Pare of the Best Plane Chamber Dogs — 6:0:0
to one Pare of Chamber Dogs £5 — 5:0:0
to one Pare of Chamber Dogs £4 — 4:0:0
to 3 Pare of the Best Brass tongs & Shovel
   at £2:10 pr Pare — 7:10:0
to 3 Pare of tongs & Shovel With Stell Legs
   at £2:10 pr Pare — 7:10:0
to 3 Pound of Roting Stone at 2/6 pr Pound — 0:7:6
                                               £89:12:6
        Cash Recd £45   45:—:—
               Ball: due £44:12:6

Recd 13th Novemr 1770 of John Cadwalader
forty four Pounds 12/6 in full of the
above Acct   pr me Danl King

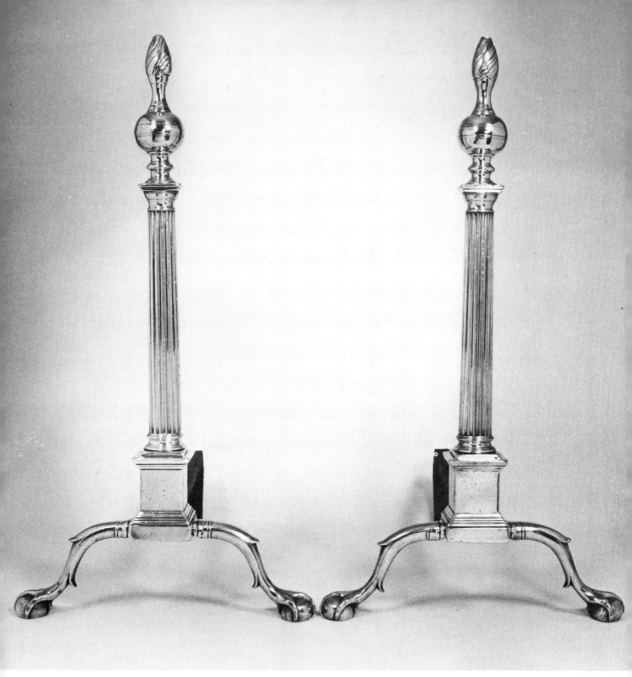

Brass andirons with cabriole legs, ball-and-claw feet, a fluted shaft and a head of a compressed ball and a twisted flame finial. They stand twenty-seven inches high. The molded legs adjoining the plinth suggest production in Philadelphia. Andirons of this style are very rare.

Bowers Collection

ANDIRONS OF THE EIGHTEENTH CENTURY

of Georgian architecture and Chippendale furniture, was exported to America. Philadelphia was rapidly becoming the most important city, certainly the most fashionable at mid-century; thus it was entirely log-

Brass andirons with cabriole legs, ball-and-claw feet, square fluted shaft, and a head of a diamond and twisted flame finial. This pattern is rare.
Bowers Collection

ical for King to incorporate the Chippendale and classical designs into his andirons. He was probably not alone in this achievement; however, the bill and a signed pair of andirons are evidences of his accomplishment.

The finials on the similar King pair seem to be incomplete, while a pair in the Bowers collection has a head in the form of a compressed ball, topped by a flame finial. It is thought that the flame finial came into popularity about mid-century and was used throughout the Chippendale period (1760–1790), but attention must be directed to other patterns of the same period.

In a spirit similar to the round fluted design, one also finds andirons with a fluted shaft, but square. The front of the pedestals are also almost square with no decoration. To the pedestals, cabriole legs are attached with spurs on the outside of the knee, terminating in the traditional ball-and-claw feet. It might be noted that neither of these Chippendale andirons has log stops mounted on top of the billet bars, nor supports under them; however, one has a crook upwards in the billet bar which functioned somewhat like a log stop.

A third important type of the Chippendale period has a pedestal mounted above a base plate to which two cabriole legs are attached. The legs have spurs on the outside at the knee, and terminate in ball-and-claw feet. The cross-sectional size of the legs is quite large on this example. The major design motif of this pattern is a twisted, fluted, vase form in the shaft which must have been quite a challenge to the two craftsmen who were involved in its production, namely, the pattern maker who carved the wooden pattern and the brass founder who rammed up the pattern in the flask and poured the brass. All examples (they are reasonably scarce) seem to be well-made as most objects of the Chippendale era were. A flat thin plate separates the shaft from the head. There is a head of a compressed vase form which is topped with a spiral fluted flame finial. The billet bars have upward crooks to keep the logs away from the column. One would naturally expect to find log stops on such a sophisticated pair of andirons, par-

Brass andirons with a twisted vase form for a shaft, topped with a head comprised of a diamond and a twisted flame finial.

Bowers Collection

One of a pair of cast iron knife-blade andirons standing beside a brass Chippendale andiron to show the similar location of the vase form on both examples. Both are rare examples of their type. They stand twenty-five inches tall.

Bowers Collection

A pair of knife blade andirons with the letters "I.C." stamped on the brass plate at the bottom of the column. Also a pair of brass andirons marked "R. Wittingham N/York" with heads similar to those on the "I.C." pair. It is concluded that I.C. as a blacksmith working in New York bought his heads from Whittingham, the brass founder. A blacksmith named John Constantine was listed in the business directories from 1795 to 1799 in New York. In the eighteenth century, the letter I was often used instead of J.

Bowers Collection

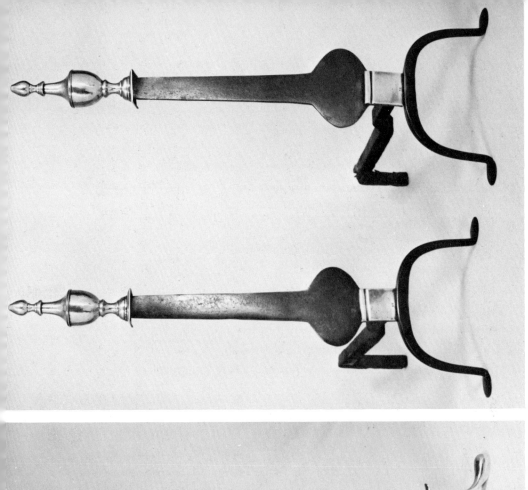

ticularly when they were used on less important examples, but there are none.

Along with these elegant brass andirons of the Chippendale period, one also finds a simple type made of wrought or cast iron, commonly called "knife blade." The origin of this term is not known, nor is it very descriptive, since the shafts do not resemble knife blades. As a matter of fact, the shafts are thin strips of iron with a silhouette suggesting a vase turning on brass Chippendale andirons.

The bulged part suggesting the vase form is usually located near the bottom of the shaft; however, one pair is known with the bulged section near the middle of the shaft, in a way paralleling the vase location on a brass andiron. Usually a flat, thin brass plate crowns the shaft, on top of which is located a number of different heads. One dominant form is the diamond, another is a compressed ball, and still another is a variety of vase forms, some of which terminate in a twisted flame.

On the bottom of the column, usually just below the bulge, a brass plate was fitted to cover the evidence that the billet bar was riveted to the vertical column. The initials I.C. were stamped on some examples; presumably they are the initials of the maker. Despite a constant search for the owner of these initials, only a tentative attribution can be made in this survey.

It has been determined that the brass heads on at least one pair of these I.C. andirons match those on a pair of brass andirons made by R. Whittingham of New York City. The logical conclusion from this observation would be that I.C. also worked in New York City. Further research reveals that a blacksmith named John Constantine worked in New York City from 1795 until 1799. Because these dates overlap those of Whittingham, and because an I. was sometimes used instead of a J., it has been tentatively concluded that the maker of the I.C. andirons was John Constantine.

By keeping an eye on the domestic architecture of the eighteenth century, one discerns that the Georgian style was slipping way in favor of the Federal. There was no evident abrupt change from one to the other, instead older styles were used along with the newer ones, particularly in andirons.

ANDIRONS OF THE EIGHTEENTH CENTURY

There were basically three sizes of andirons used in the last decade of the eighteenth century. One was a tall pattern (24 inches tall) with a cabriole leg, ball-and-claw or penny feet, and a pedestal frequently rectangular rather than the earlier square. The pedestal was kept

Typical tall andirons of the 1790–1800 era.

Bowers Collection

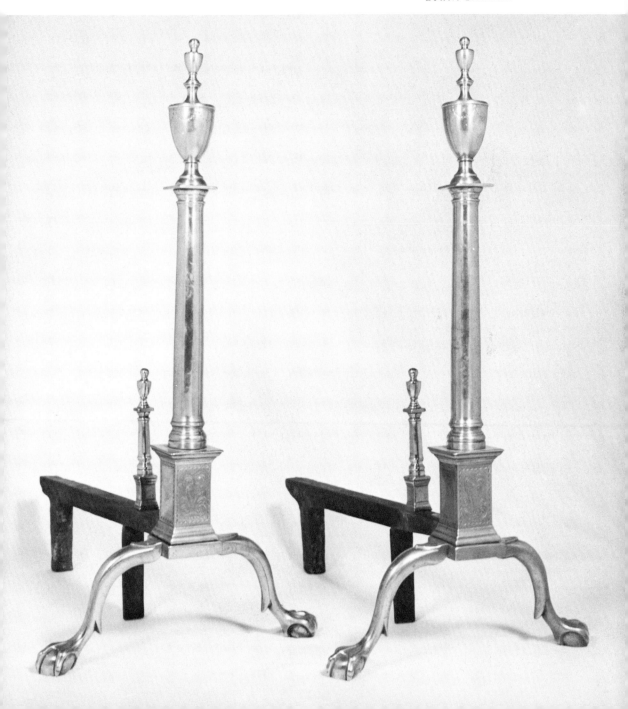

rigidly in place by fitting down over the legs, and there were sometimes escallops in the front edge of the plinth. The front surface of the pedestals was sometimes engraved with motifs such as weeping willows (thought to be a symbol of mourning), and eagles.

The length of the shaft was not reduced, however, and there were many more smooth ones than ones with flutes. The shaft was topped with heads such as acorns and lemons, but most frequently by a classical urn. Some of the urns have beaded edges, following a detail found on pewter and silver objects of the period.

Although there are hundreds of this example, the most interesting documentation of its period is found in an invoice of John Bailey, a New York brass founder, coppersmith, silversmith, and iron monger, dated November 5, 1790. In the upper left hand corner of this invoice is illustrated an andiron fitting the description above. The attractive appearance and plentiful supply of these andirons caused them to be used with earlier furnishings.

A second pattern of andiron used in the decade of the 1790's was similar to the tall type, but was only about eighteen inches tall. Because they were shorter, the pedestal became almost square again as seen in a pair made by T. Brooks of Philadelphia, who died in 1798. This type is not plentiful, and most of them lack the charm of their taller brothers. It is particularly interesting to note that at least one tall pair is known to have been shortened to meet the fashion for shorter andirons. This trend was nurtured by the fact that at this time fireplaces were becoming smaller, and the early long models could not be used in them.

The third andiron pattern of the period was a short, squat type in which the shaft was eliminated, with a consequent enlargement of the pedestal and the head. The heads continued in the shape of urns, acorns, and lemons, and some are engraved. Some pedestals are also

Semi-tall brass andirons made by T. Brooks, Philadelphia. The signature is on the bottom plate, covered by the pedestal as shown in insert. This is a very uncommon place to sign andirons.
Bowers Collection

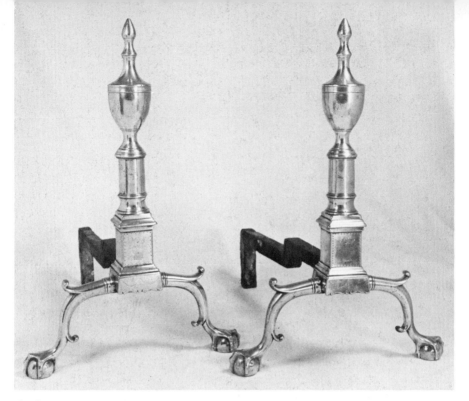

Andirons with shortened shafts.

Bowers Collection

engraved. Most examples have cabriole legs with ball-and-claw or penny feet.

At this point, a word might be said about the manner in which andirons of the eighteenth century were made and held together. In most examples, the legs and the bottom plate joining them were cast in one piece. This procedure required a clever bit of maneuvering to get the complicated and undercut pattern out of the sand without disturbing the intricate details of the ball-and-claw foot. The shaft and pedestal were cast in sections and joined by brazing them together, after which they were filed and fitted to each other as was also the head.

The front end of the billet bar was forged flat and spread sidewise. A hole was punched in the middle of the plate joining the feet and the wide end of the billet bar. Through these holes, a forged bar was placed with an offset just above the billet bar to keep the assembly in place after the iron bar was riveted on the bottom. This iron bar extended upward through the pedestal and the shaft so that it extended above the top level of the shaft. There the head was fitted and attached, in early times by riveting the center bar, in later times by using a thread. If a thread was used, the parts could be easily disassembled.

Before threading, the inner iron bar was forged into an agreeable shape to facilitate the threading operation. The threads are usually coarse and not sharply cut as with modern tools. Fine sharp threads are strong suggestions that the bar has been recut or the andiron is not an original of the period.

Low, squat andirons of the 1790's with engraved heads. This is a reasonably attractive example of this type of andiron. Notice the grooves filed on the top of the billet bar.

Kauffman Collection

An unassembled andiron of the eighteenth century. The shaft is made of four pieces cast separately and then brazed together at the corners. This procedure makes the joints virtually invisible.

Bowers Collection

Care must be exercised in taking andirons apart, for if they haven't been disassembled for many years, the threads might be corroded and the inner bar twisted off before the parts separate. A modern nut on the bottom of the iron bar is also evidence that the piece is probably a reproduction. These comments are made not to imply that reproductions are inferior, but that one should know if one is purchasing a "period" piece or a reproduction. It is also wise to bear in mind that reproductions have been made over a long span of years and are sometimes difficult to identify.

It is necessary to keep an eye on the andirons and the architecture of the late eighteenth century house and also on the fireplace. At approximately the turn of the century, a major alteration occurred in the size and shape of the fireplaces, with a corresponding modification in the size and style of the andirons. Reference has already been made to the change in the size of the fireplace, namely, the gradual but persistent reduction in the size of the fire chamber. This brought about variations in the decor around the fireplace, not so much in style as in the critical matter of size. It is obvious that regardless of the style, the early large andirons could not be used without difficulty, if at all, in the later small fire chambers.

The whole crux of the problem at the turn of the nineteenth century was the implementation of new concepts advanced by Count Rumford, originally an American citizen, who spent most of his life in various countries of Europe. Rumford was an ingenious experimenter, one of the first to recognize that the fireplaces of the eighteenth century were quite inefficient in dispensing heat. The earlier fire chambers were large, and the walls were flat and square with each other; thus, there was very little projection of heat into the room in which the fireplace was located. It is possible Rumford got his clue for the recommended changes from the construction of the Franklin fireplace, which Franklin had perfected in the 1740's. At least, his flaring side walls (called jambs) could have been copied directly. However, there does not appear to be any precedent for his slanting back wall of the fireplace. With all the walls slanting inward, the fireplace became a much more efficient unit, and the fire chamber could be made smaller. This obviously resulted in a great saving of heat and use of wood, now becoming scarce in the big cities. Andirons became shorter than those of the Chippendale era.

This last statement should not lead one to the conclusion that all andirons were smaller, at least those in the middle of the Federal era. Whittingham is known to have made some of his "double lemon" styles which were twenty-six inches high. Likewise, frugality dictated that owners of tall andirons would try to fit them into smaller fire chambers. As a matter of fact, it has been mentioned that one example is known to have been cut off to make a shorter shaft and replace the finial.

The matter of the relative size of the andiron in relation to the fireplace opening might be regarded as a debatable question. There is obviously a definite limit to the height of the andirons. If they are very tall and reach to the lintel of the fireplace, the placing of logs within the chamber will be difficult indeed, almost impossible. There is no limit as far as the use of short ones is concerned; some less than half the height of the opening are usable, but obviously inadequate from an esthetic point of view. There is no hard and fast rule about this matter. From the writer's point of view, however, andirons which are about two-thirds the height of the opening seem to be a practical size and look reasonably well-proportioned.

It might also be pointed out that some fireplace openings in bedrooms were as small as two feet by two feet. These would utilize very small andirons, and there are adequate examples surviving that would be usable in such a small opening. Very few are noted for the beauty and grace of their lines. There are exceptions such as the hairy paw ones in Winterthur, but no others of importance equating these.

A point was made in the discussion of Federal andirons of the late eighteenth century that they were basically styled in the Chippendale manner, that is, the shafts were tall; they had cabriole legs, and penny or ball-and-claw feet.

In summary, it might be observed that andirons of the early eighteenth century retained some of the primitive elements of the seventeenth century such as straight columns and trestle feet. These primitive elements were slowly replaced by the sophisticated forms of the Queen Anne and Chippendale styles, namely, cabriole legs, tall fluted shafts, and twisted flame finials. The connoisseur of today regards these styles as almost beyond improvement, but not so with the gentry of the period. Man seems to have an insatiable whim for change, and hopefully improvement, but it is doubtful if the quality of andiron design was raised in the nineteenth century. The writers of this survey regard the eighteenth century as one of great achievement, and there is some substance to the concept that the eighteenth century was the Golden Era of decorative arts in America.

CHAPTER IV

Andirons of the Nineteenth Century

LOOKING backward to the andirons of the late eighteenth century, it is evident that it was a time of transition in andiron styles. Shortened andirons were being made to fit smaller fireplace openings of the period; however, elements of the earlier tall andirons were still evident. The next step was to lay aside the surviving details and start anew.

The era for the new styles of andirons can be ascertained in two ways. First, a number of craftsmen working at this time signed their products, and, second, by this time large cities on the eastern seacoast had published business directories, particularly Boston, New York, and Philadelphia. Two of the most important brass founders of the era were John Bailey and Richard Whittingham, Sr., both of whom worked in New York City. About fifty examples are known bearing the Whittingham signature, and possibly a dozen are known to be products of Bailey. In addition, there was T. Brooks of Philadelphia, who died in 1798; John Molineux, J. Davis, the Hunnemans of Boston, and Charles Weir of Baltimore.

Although a low height was one of the main characteristics of the new breed of andirons, some of the new patterns were reasonably tall. There are examples of the "double lemon" pattern that are as tall as twenty-six inches. The production of tall ones can simply be explained by the fact that although fireplaces were being made smaller, there were many large ones remaining which needed tall andirons. Despite the tall examples, the general trend was toward shorter andirons.

Imprint of the name "Molineux" on the brass plate which covers part of the billet bar. The name "Boston" was placed in front of the log stop, only the "N" can be seen in this photograph. Notice the attractive design filed in the end of the brass plate.

Kauffman Collection

The cross-sectional shape of the pedestals was square, round, or hexagonal. On the square examples, an escalloped skirt sometimes extended below the plinth on the front, the sides were sometimes fitted with a small half-round opening to fit over the legs, and the back was accommodated to fit the billet bar.

A variety of heads and finials were used such as the double lemon (a big one with a smaller one on top), a ball and spool top, vase, and the famous ball and steeple. The ball and steeple were popular in Boston and New York, both Molineux and Davis using it in Boston and Whittingham in New York. The Whittinghams and Bailey also used the ball and spool motif. The principal parts other than the legs are hollow and were cast in separate sections as in earlier times. Designs made by

J. Davis and Whittingham were generally excellent and the workmanship superb. However, as the old masters died, design and workmanship showed signs of deterioration, and after 1820 a fast decline set in as Empire motifs took over, and interest in fine hand workmanship declined with the coming of the machine age.

A rather obvious innovation was a change in style of legs and feet. At the turn of the century a modification of the cabriole leg was made with the introduction of additional spurs and the use of ball feet, the latter being popular with New York makers. Pad feet returned as well as the "snake" foot with a ridged top, reminiscent of earlier Queen Anne styling. A notable quality of the snake feet popular in Boston is the fact that they were hollowed out in the back, apparently to save metal and the amount of finishing required by the maker. The cabriole legs used

An unusually short pair of knife blade andirons. These were either cut shorter for use in a small fireplace, or always were short. The urn head suggests they were made in the era of short andirons.

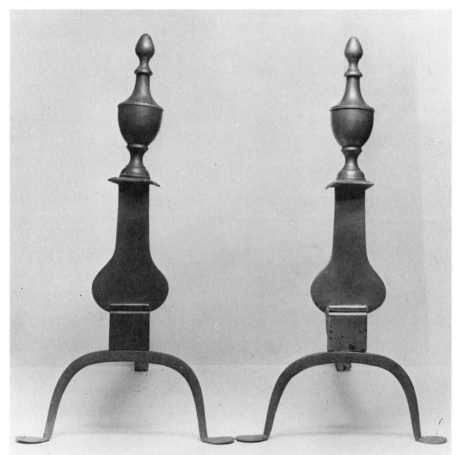

Disassembled andiron made by J. Davis of Boston at the turn of the century. The fine craftsmanship of Davis is evident in his product.

Bowers Collection

A very fine pair of brass andirons made by R. Whittingham of New York. In addition to the galleries, these have octagonal pedestals and the new legs of the period.

Bowers Collection

A typical pair of andirons made by Hunneman of Boston, and a set of firetools with matching finials marked "Boston." It is very likely that Hunneman also made the firetools.

Courtesy Tenia Baunstone

with the ball feet extended out over the ball, and ended in pointed tips or sometimes ended with a vertical drop to the ball, a feature found on some mid-eighteenth century iron baluster type andirons with brass heads. This design was used considerably by R. Whittingham. Marked Boston andirons have vertical log stops and rectangular billet bars, whereas examples from New York, Philadelphia, and Baltimore have square billet bars with a vertical offset to prevent the log from rolling forward.

One of the unique achievements in the design of andirons of the period was the introduction of "rights" and "lefts." These were more decorative than the straight designs and could be set on the outside of a shallow fireplace on the front of the hearth and spread quite widely in a very

Pair of typical brass andirons of the Empire era.

Courtesy Bradley Antiques

decorative manner. Some of these andirons were fitted with pierced brass galleries or wing-fenders which are highly decorative as well as functional. Most examples have four legs, two in the front, one at the point where the billet bar breaks from its curve and extends backwards, and finally, one at the rear end. These all have log stops which are a part of the decorative scheme. This innovation did not change the function of andirons but made them more prestigious looking.

By 1820, most of the old craftsmen had died, retired, or turned to other work. The Hunnemans, however, continued to make andirons composed of a turned column in front, without feet, a second turned column with a foot, at the bend in the billet bar, and the third foot at the back end where the billet bar was bent downward. The Hunnemans also made andirons in the traditional style of their period, but their fame rests largely on the fact that they signed and *numbered* many of their products. These strange-looking andirons without feet were apparently first made by John Molineux early in the nineteenth century when he was a very old man.

The downward trend in the design of andirons continued into the Empire period. These have a slight relevance to the furniture of the period, but their name is derived largely on the basis that they were contemporary with the furniture. The most persistent pattern consisted of a turned column ranging in height from about ten inches to thirty. This column was very thick for its height, and was divided into many short unrelated areas. By looking at the diameter, one would expect to find columns much taller than they really are. The unfortunate large diameter would seem to be enough distortion, but these columns were mounted on thin spindle-like legs terminating in feet of one or two balls. Some of these do not have the vertical joint found in earlier examples, and one can conclude from the lack of joint that they were cast hollow with a "core" and no joint was necessary.

In the evolution of styles in any area, there is often a recurrence of motifs and/or materials. It is very interesting to note that the first and last andirons used in America were made of cast iron; however, there was a marked difference in the styles. The earliest andirons were massive and heavy with a minimum of decoration. Those of the Victorian

Andirons of cast iron by Savery & Co. of Philadelphia. The form seems to have been inspired by the spires of a Gothic cathedral. This style was obviously appropriate for the architecture and furnishings of the Victorian era.

Courtesy The Henry Ford Museum, Dearborn, Michigan

era were much smaller, and thus, much lighter in weight. They seem to be composed of nothing but decorative motifs, and their "gingerbread" style seems entirely appropriate to be used with the architecture and furnishings of the era. There were also fenders of cast iron.

A complete directory of men who made andirons will never be possible; however, herewith is a list of those known to the authors at this time.

MAKERS OF BRASS ANDIRONS

Name	Location	Working Date
Allison, Peter	New York, N.Y.	1804
Bailey, John	New York, N.Y.	1778
Brooks, Thomas	Philadelphia, Pa.	1797
Carr, Robert	New York, N.Y.	1820
Clark, John	Boston, Mass.	1789
Davis, James	Boston, Mass.	1803
Edmands, Barnabas	Charlestown, Mass.	1799
Griffiths & Morgans	New York, N.Y.	1832
Hunneman, William C.	Boston, Mass.	1797
King, Daniel	Philadelphia, Pa.	1770
Molineux, John	Boston, Mass.	1806
Norton, T.	unknown	unknown
Noyes & Cummings	Salem, Mass.	unknown
Noyes, John	Bangor, Maine	unknown
Phillips, David	New York, N.Y.	1815
Smylie, Edward	New York, N.Y.	1830
Stickney, John	Boston, Mass.	1820
Stimson, John	Boston, Mass.	1830
Tuston, W.	Philadelphia, Pa.	1811
Wallace, Robert	New York, N.Y.	1802
Webb, William Holmes	Warren, Maine	1799
Weir, Charles	Baltimore, Md.	1796
Whittingham, Richard	New York, N.Y.	1794

ADVERTISERS WHO MADE BRASS ANDIRONS

Name	Location	Working Date
Baker, Joseph	New York, N.Y.	1801
Baxter, Isaac	Philadelphia, Pa.	1831
Belcher, Joseph	Newport, R.I.	unknown

Name	Location	Working Date
Caustin, Isaac	Philadelphia, Pa.	1791
Getty, David & Wm.	Williamsburg, Va.	1751
Gregory, Thomas	Philadelphia, Pa.	1819
Hedderly, Richard	Philadelphia, Pa.	1819
Jackson, Mary	Boston, Mass.	1736
Kip, James	Fishkill, New York	1782
Leaycraft, Richard	Fishkill, New York	1793
Servoss, C. K.	Philadelphia, Pa.	1831
Smith, James	Philadelphia, Pa.	1753
Syng, Philip	Annapolis, Md.	1759
Wareham, John	New York, N.Y.	1793
Zane & Chapman	Philadelphia, Pa.	1792

MAKERS OF IRON ANDIRONS

Name	Location	Working Date
Ball, L.	unknown	unknown
I. C.	New York, N.Y. ?	1795
Crammer, H. D.	unknown	unknown
Starr, N.	Middletown, Conn.	1800
Steel, John	Philadelphia, Pa.	1818
Turle, I.	unknown	unknown
Webb, Joseph *	Boston, Mass.	late 18th century

* Webb's products are identified from illustrations on his trade card.

CHAPTER V

Fenders and Grates

BECAUSE they are, next to andirons, the most important accessories of the American fireplace, we have put these two items in a separate chapter instead of including them in the alphabetical listing of accessories in Chapter VIII.

FENDERS

Fenders seem to have been used first in the seventeenth century. The earliest examples were simply made of sheet iron by turning over an edge on which the fender could rest and not fall over. There was little or no ornamentation. Such an object could be appropriately used in the house of an English yeoman, or a colonist in Virginia or Massachusetts. The type is described by Dionysius Lardner in his *Cabinet Encyclopedia*, Vol. II, London, 1833.

> The first fenders were mere bent pieces of sheet iron, placed in front of the fire, to prevent brands, or cinders, from rolling off the hearthstone upon wooden floors. These common articles were, in the first place, either blackened, painted or polished, according to the means of the purchaser. Fashion and ingenuity, however, presently combined in the production of that elegant and standard ornament of the hearth, the polished cut steel fender.

With the coming of more sophisticated houses in the eighteenth century, the style and material of fenders changed. Doubtless some continued to be made of iron; however, a more easy access to brass

Brass serpentine fender of the Federal era, ornamented with three eagles. One expert who made a long study of fenders believed that the "returns" on the ends of such fenders identified them as products of American craftsmen.

Courtesy The Metropolitan Museum of Art, Kennedy Fund, 1918

caused many to be formed of cast brass. A number of sections were cast, which were attached and formed into a serpentine shape. The evidence of the technique is an unfinished surface on the inner side of the fender. This type is usually about six or eight inches high and profusely ornamented. The technology of the nineteenth century brought another production mode to the making of fenders, namely, the use of the "fly-press." Lardner comments further about this procedure.

> The rich and open work exhibited in some of these wares (fenders) is produced by means of the fly-press, in the following ingenious manner: the plate (sheet), whether of brass or steel, having been prepared by rolling and planishing, to the proper strength, and cut with shears to the size required, is brought to the piercing shop.

Thereafter follows a long and detailed account of the insertion of a male and female die on the fly-press, on top of which is mounted a long bar (handle) with a ball of metal attached to each end. The

The appearance of sets with matching parts suggests that at times such sets were made by craftsmen making andirons. The fenders varied in height; however, this example is about average. This set was made about the turn of the nineteenth century.

Courtesy Schiffer Antiques

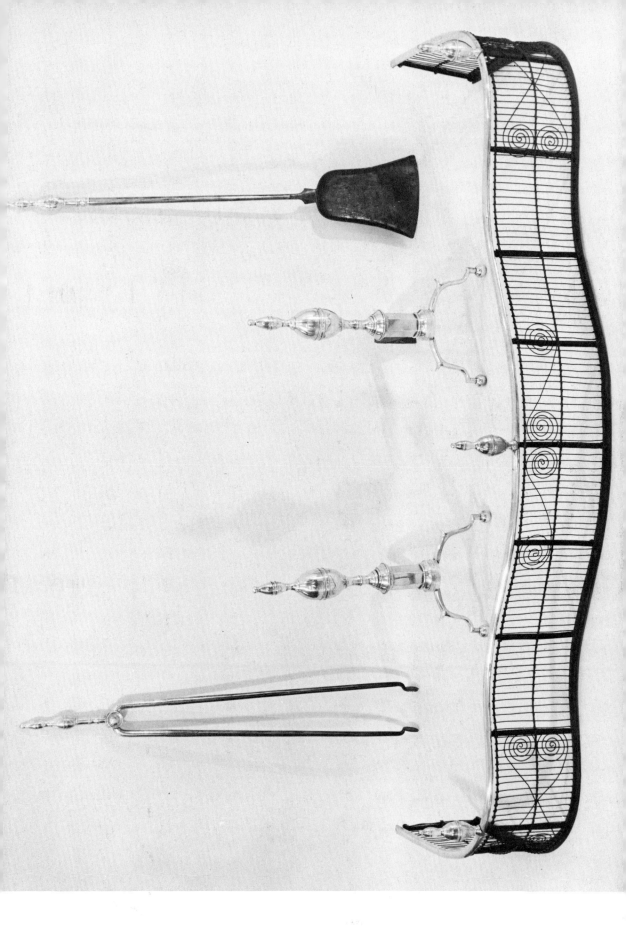

sheet metal was inserted in the press, the handle spun with the balls giving it increased momentum, and piercings made in a section of the intended fender. This process was repeated until the entire length had been appropriately pierced. Lardner comments about the finishing process.

> The plate is then planished or levelled by hammering, after which it is sent to the grinding wheel to be got up on the stone, and afterwards it is polished with emery and crocus in a manner similar to the getting up of cutlery. The piercing of brass-faced fenders is effected exactly in the same manner as the perforation of the iron ones: the mode of getting up is likewise similar, only that the brass fronts, are, when flat, buffed on a leather-covered wheel with sand, and when fluted they are brushed with rotten-stone and oil. The plates, previously plain or straight, are then bent into the shape desired, and the fender is finished by riveting a tube of brass drawn upon an iron rod, along the top; and, in like manner, by affixing of a moulding or plinth of brass upon the bottom, and then placing underneath the fender a plate of rolled iron. The whole is usually supported upon four lacquered claws or ball feet.

A survey of fenders will quickly disclose that in addition to sheet metal, some were made principally of short pieces of iron wire, attached at the top and bottom ends to a rod of iron to make the arrangement rigid and useful. These, being as high as eighteen inches, were designed to not only prevent coals from rolling onto the floor, but also to prevent sparks from flying into the room. Lardner's description of these follows:

> A variety of fenders, composed chiefly of reticulated wirework, having moulded tops and bottoms of bright metal, have been introduced; some of these have a light and elegant appearance; but as they do not admit to being conveniently cleaned, they are much seldomer composed of polished than of painted wire. This description of articles is more particularly adapted to those situations in which it is necessary to screen the fire, as a provision against the danger to be apprehended from the flying about of hot cinders, the approach of children, etc.

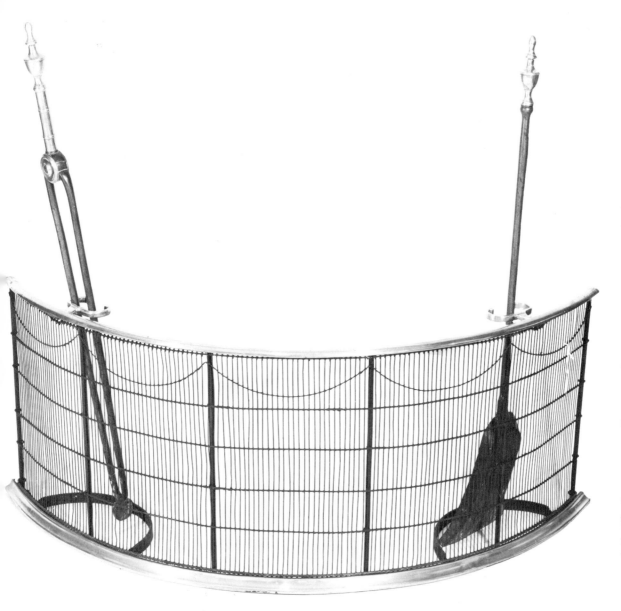

An unusual fender of the nineteenth century with jamb hooks added. These hooks for holding tools were usually fastened to the jambs of the fireplace. This fender is fifteen inches high.

Courtesy Schiffer Antiques

A final type of fender is made up principally of vertical iron bars instead of wire, ranging from eighteen to thirty inches high. Those about eighteen inches high often have a seat mounted on the top edge for people to sit by the fire. These are called "club fenders." The taller type are called "nursery fenders." Lardner also comments about them.

> The numerous and fatal accidents occurring to children and others, in consequence of their approaching too near the bars of an open fireplace, have led to the adoption of screens and other contrivances having more or less the character of fenders, and calculated to fence the burning fuel.

When one examines much of the fireplace equipment in the antique shops of the 1960's and 70's, it becomes very apparent that vast quantities of fenders were made in Britain and exported to America. This situation was true in the eighteenth century as well. Many iron mongers of Boston, New York, and Philadelphia advertised the fact that they had recently received a fresh shipment of such goods from abroad, usually England. The constant practice of American craftsmen copying English designs has made it virtually impossible for the locally made examples to be distinguished from those imported. Some American craftsmen, however, advertised the manufacture of fenders here. The famous Mary Jackson advertised fenders as one of the products of her shop in Boston. The following advertisement appeared in *The Boston Gazette*, Sept. 27/Oct. 4, 1736.

> BRAZIERS' WARES.—Mary Jackson, at the Brazen-Head, in Cornhill, makes and sells all sorts of Brass Founders Ware; as Hearths, Fenders, Shovels, Brasses for Chaises and Saddles, of the newest fashion; all sorts of polished Brazier's Ware, at reasonable rates. A Quantity of Large brown Paper fit for sheathing ships, to be Sold: Likewise buys old Copper, Brass, Pewter, Lead and Iron.

GRATES

Next to andirons, the grate was the most important accessory of the fireplace in America. From this book's point of view, they have been "short changed" in the history of decorative arts in America.

This condition arises from the fact that grates reached the zenith of their use in the mid-nineteenth century, a time not highly regarded by contemporary connoisseurs. In the "long run" this prejudice will be overcome, and grates will reach their rightful place in the history of decorative arts in America. In the 1830's, approximately seventy-five craftsmen and merchants, in New York City alone, were selling grates, which makes them important on the basis of numbers, regardless of their attractiveness.

Their appeal at mid-nineteenth century lies in the fact that they became very fashionable; their "splashy" array of metals made them shine in the fireplace, and they obviously were more efficient in heating a room than the old-fashioned andirons. By that time, the throat of the fireplace was greatly reduced in size, which meant that with a grate in the fireplace less heat went up the chimney and more was projected into the room. They had another virtue, namely, the vast majority of them were suited to the burning of coal. Although this was a dirty fuel to handle, the quantity involved was small, and receptacles were designed to contain the coal on the hearth, and in the "long run" the hearth was a more spic and span place than formerly when wood was burned. But a desire for change alone could account for the rejection of andirons and the acceptance of grates. Thus, it can be truthfully said that the caprice of humanity could account for their popularity, regardless of their virtues and liabilities.

Although grates were most widely used in the mid-nineteenth century, it is very evident that they were used in America as early as the 1730's. At that time, advertisements appeared in Boston newspapers telling that grates were for sale, presumably by private owners who for one reason or another wanted to dispose of them. This procedure might be explained by the fact that English emigrants had equipped their fireplaces with them in England, but when they saw the virtues of using andirons in America, they wished to dispose of their grates. These grates were probably made in England, for at that time the limited use of grates in America would not have warranted a trade of "grate making" here, their small size also being an inducement for importing them from abroad. The securing of coal in America at that time might also have been a problem; however,

wood and peat could also have been burned in them. At first coal was imported from England to use in the grates, but in 1762, banks of coal were discovered near the present site of Wilkes Barre, Pennsylvania. Its slow burning and excellent production of heat caused it to become slowly accepted until the mid-nineteenth century. By the 1830's, Franklin Fireplaces were equipped with coal burning grates, and for awhile there must have been some competition between Franklin Fireplaces and coal burning grates. The higher cost of the fireplaces gave an edge to grates and, of course, they finally won. Their success was short-lived, for by mid-century stoves were rapidly becoming fashionable, and the once fashionable grate became a vestige of an earlier age.

With the foregoing historical perspective of the grate, some consideration should be given to the technological aspects of its installation and use. Like many other devices, the grate had to have an entrepreneur. In this case, at least one of them was Count Rumford, an American living abroad, but his ideas must have filtered rapidly back to America, for they were very wise and practical, two virtues Americans have been known for from the very start. At the same time (early 1790's) Rumford published plans for making a fireplace more efficient in the production of heat, but the concern here will be only with his ideas about grates.

Rumford's major premise about fireplaces was that they should be reduced in size for burning wood, and he further recommended that they be still smaller for the installation of grates. Presumably the small size for grates was based on the premise that they were more efficient in the production of heat. He suggested that the border between the small grate and the former big fireplace opening be filled with masonry materials, because they were cheap, very flexible, and

An early basket-type grate of wrought iron standing in the fireplace of the family dining room of the Governor's Palace in Williamsburg, Virginia. An iron fireback is standing between the grate and the back wall of the fireplace to protect the soft bricks from disintegrating.

Courtesy Colonial Williamsburg

highly satisfactory for the purpose. He pointed out that the use of metals was to be avoided because they absorb heat rather than reflect it. Some of his specific directions for fitting grates were put forth in the early 1790's, and were as follows:

> In placing the grate, the thing principally to be attended to, is to make the back of it coincide with the back of the Fireplace;—as many of the grates in common use will be found to be too large. When the Fireplaces are altered and improved, it will be necessary to diminish their capacities by filling up the back and the sides with pieces of fire-stone. When this is done, it is the front of the flat piece of fire-stone which is made to form a new back for the grate, which must coincide with, and make part of the back of the Fire-place. But in diminishing the capacities of the grates with pieces of fire-stone, care must be taken not to make them *too narrow.*
>
> The proper width for grates destined for rooms of a middling size will be from six to eight inches, and their lengths may be diminished more or less, according to the room to be heated with more or less difficulty, or as the weather is more or less severe. But where the width of a grate is not more than five inches, it will be very difficult to prevent the fire from going out.

Rumford then points out that if the large size of the grate causes a problem in installing it, he recommends that the back of the grate be removed and the three-sided iron basket be attached to the back wall of the fireplace. This procedure was probably the start of the change from a portable grate to one that was permanently installed. If the opening for the grate be very small, its size could be enlarged for holding coal. Semicircular bars could be placed one above another to the desired height. He points out that it was easier to adapt the grate to the fireplace than vice versa.

He then illustrates his suggestions in a series of drawings, nos. 7, 8, 9. His comments are as follows:

UNITED STATES PATENT OFFICE.

ROGER M. SHERMAN, OF FAIRFIELD, CONNECTICUT.

OPEN FIREPLACE OR GRATE.

Specification of Letters Patent No. 249, dated June 30, 1837.

To all whom it may concern:

Be it known that I, ROGER M. SHERMAN, of Fairfield, in the county of Fairfield and State of Connecticut, have invented Improvements in Open Fireplaces or Grates, of which the following is a description.

This stove or grate consists of the following parts, as represented in the annexed drawing—first, an open fireplace (a) of cast or sheet iron, or any suitable material, lined with firebrick, soapstone, or other proper nonconductor of heat, with a grate (b) for fuel. The dimensions of this fireplace may be varied as circumstances require. I will assume that it is eighteen inches wide and three feet high. On each side is a jamb or pillar ($c, c,$) supporting a mantel piece ($d,$) over the fireplace, in the form in which parlor grates, for anthracite coal, are often made. This mantel piece constitutes the front of an open chamber into which the heat and smoke ascend, and thence pass up through the flues into the radiators; the back and ends of the chamber being closed. This structure is surmounted by several hollow radiators (1, 2, 3,) extending from side to side in a position about parallel with each other and with the chamber, and, in a stove of the dimensions here assumed about two inches apart, and six inches in width by three in depth. There are three flues ($h, h, h,$) between the chamber and the first or lowest radiator; one in the middle, which is about half the width of the fireplace (or nine inches in this stove) and one at each end of half the same width, by which the heat and smoke are conducted from the chamber into the first radiator. The number of radiators may be varied at pleasure. They are connected, successively, by three flues, passing from each to the next, of the same dimensions and structure as those already described ($j, j, j, k, k, k.$)

From the back of the chamber, passing into the chimney of the apartment where the stove is set, or other avenue for carrying off the smoke, is a flue ($l,$) called the direct flue, which has a valve or damper ($u,$) close to the chamber, by which it is opened or closed at pleasure. This flue ought to be of the same width as the fireplace, and of sufficient capacity. When open, it causes a strong draft, and kindles the fire. When closed, the heat and smoke ascend into the radiators.

Passing out of the back side of the upper radiator, at its center, is a flue called the back flue ($m,$) which descends so as to enter the direct flue beyond its damper, as at p. If there are three radiators above the chamber, as in the annexed drawing, valves or dampers should be interposed in particular flues in the following manner; one in the middle flue, ($n,$) below the first radiator; one in each of the end flues between the first and second radiators, ($s, s,$) and one in the middle flue ($t,$) between the second and third radiators. By closing these valves, after the fire is kindled, the stove will have its greatest power; and by them the heat may be regulated at pleasure. If the location is favorable to a strong draft, the back flue, especially if the stove is small, or if there is but one radiator, may pass directly into the chimney, and no direct flue will be necessary. The stove should be placed a little distance from the wall, so as to permit the air to pass freely behind it.

The object of this invention is to unite, in the manner described, a pleasant, open fireplace, with the warmth and economy of the close stove. The stove and radiator may be made to present a handsome perpendicular front, susceptible of any degree of ornament. It may be adapted to the use of any kind of fuel. Sheet iron is a proper material for the radiators. Their ends should be made in the form of caps, to be taken off at pleasure, for the purpose of cleaning them of soot. The radiators, in like manner, may be separated at the flues for the same purpose.

All I claim as my invention, and for which I ask Letters Patent, is—

The combination of the open fireplace with the radiators placed over it horizontally, connected by several flues with the chamber, and with each other, as aforesaid.

Dated at Fairfield, Connecticut, the 8th day of June A. D. 1837.

ROGER M. SHERMAN.

Witnesses:
THOMAS B. COBORNE,
JEREMIAH T. DENISON.

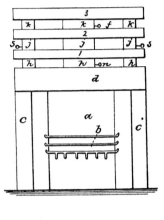

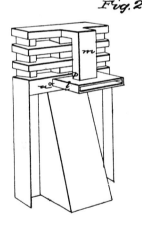

Illustrations and a description of a coal grate patented June 30, 1837, by R. M. Sherman. The numbers 1, 2 and 3 indicated radiators of sheet iron (really smoke chambers) which assisted in disseminating heat.

Courtesy United States Patent Office

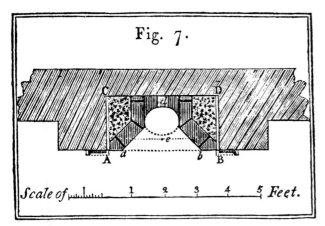 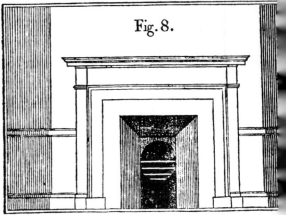

Figure 7. This figure represents the ground plan of a Chimney Fireplace in which the grate is placed in a nich, and in which the original width A B of the Fire-place is considerably diminished. a b is the opening of the Fire-place in front after it has been altered, and is the back of the nich in which the grate is placed. (The nich is necessary for the altered fire-place does not have adequate depth to have it function satisfactorily.)

Fig. 8. Shows a front view of the same Fire-place after it has been altered; where may be seen the grate, and the doorway for the Chimney-sweeper.

Fig. 9. Shows a section of the same Fire-place, c d e, being a section of the nich, g the door-way for the Chimney-sweeper, closed by a piece of firestone, and of the New wall under the mantel by which the height of the Fire-place in front is diminished.

It should be noted that the fire chamber in his design is raised considerably above the level of the hearth. He does not explain the reason for such a procedure; however, subsequent designers made a point of lowering the fire closer to or on the hearth. Rumford might have been concerned with keeping the fire near the throat of the fireplace, for such an action minimized the chances of the apparatus sending smoke into the room instead of up the chimney. Rumford not only had many ideas, he was a prolific writer, and his plans were circulated widely. The source of this information is *Essays, Political, Economical, and Philosophical,* Volume I, printed by W. Porter, 69 Grafton Street, and J. Archer, 80 Dame-Street, Dublin, 1796.

The desire for a better apparatus for heating rooms, in conjunction with the demand for innovative technological devices, caused many men to experiment with ideas concerned with heating. Many ideas

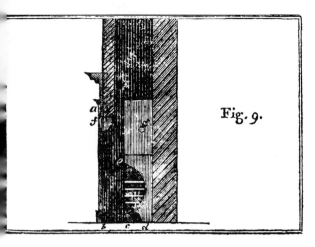

Fig. 9.

are recorded in *The Open Fireplace* by James R. Osgood, printed in Boston in 1882. At least two plans utilized the ideas advanced by a man named Sylvester, who suggested the following:

> The bottom of the grate was formed of separate bars, which extended considerably into the room. A curb of iron and a raised bar or circular form was used to inclose the bars (which were lying flat on the hearth), and answer the purpose of a fender. The back and sides of the fireplace were formed of brick. Instead of the register door above, Venetian plates were provided at the back of the grate for the escape of smoke, which could be opened more or less by a touch of a poker....
>
> The contraction of the Chimney-throat by means of the Venetian plates, which could be easily regulated, was an excellent application of the principle advocated by Rumford. The projecting bars reflected considerable heat, but there were certain disadvantages. The apparatus was necessarily expensive. The fire was judiciously low, and the necessitating of removing the bars individually for the purpose of taking away the dust, and of then replacing them, was objected to, from the fact that the operation was an unusual one, and one, therefore, which domestics (bless their soul) were certain to object to.

The last design to be considered here for a grate was one which was placed on a moveable carriage, with wheels or coasters which allowed the grate to be brought forward into the room after the fire was started and chances for undue amounts of smoke minimized. One of these was fitted with telescoping tubes, which carried the smoke

Empire styled grate with a facade made largely of brass. Although keeping the brass bright was a chore, the result was probably worth the effort.

Courtesy Edwin Jackson

back into the chimney after the carriage was brought forward. This plan, of course, demanded a large protruding hearth, but irregularities such as this were easily tolerated if the result brought more heat into the room. Bringing this device clear to the back wall caused convectional currents of heat to circulate in the room and heat more thoroughly than a device which depended entirely on radiation of heat.

Throughout the nineteenth century, many American fireplaces were fitted with grates, some of which Rumford would approve; others he would not. An endless number of forms were used in building the grates; some were fitted permanently and some were free-standing.

FENDERS AND GRATES

Probably most of them can be identified as the product of a known maker; however, to the writers' knowledge no list of American grate makers is known to exist.

In order to start a documented list of American grate makers, the writers have listed the names of about seventy-five men who worked in New York City in the first half of the nineteenth century. It should be noted that no grate makers were found to be working in

A style of frame and grate popular in America, ca. 1840–50. This type of an arrangement obviously has to be backed with a masonry wall. The black portions are of sheet iron with contrasting ornaments of pewter.
Courtesy Edwin Jackson

the eighteenth century. This statement does not imply that there were none at that early time, but that none were known *per se* as grate makers. The use of grates in America as early as the 1730's suggests that some were made here, but not enough to qualify a man as primarily a grate maker. Of course, it is more likely that ones used in the early times in America were imported from Britain; however, some of the early ones were simply baskets made of wrought iron, and any blacksmith could have made one. In the nineteenth century, many were made of cast iron with ornamental brass parts such as plates and finials; hence many were made by brass founders. The following names have been excerpted from the unpublished thesis of Henry Parrot Bascot, Jr., entitled *Brass Founding in New York City 1786 to 1840*. All the names were taken from documented sources; the active dates are all approximate, on the premise that these men were working before or later than their dates indicated in the records.

Craftsman	*Active date*
Ayres & Combs	1835–1839
Althause, Samuel B.	1838–1850
Austin, Benjamin	1839–1850
Birdsall, Benjamin	1814–1843
Brady, Terence	1835–1843
Brickley, William	1817–1860
Carson, Alfred	1840–1860
Clayton, Benajah	1835–1836
Clayton, High	1835–1836
Combs, Henry	1840–1843
Cook & Hampton	1828–1830
Conroe, Michael	1836–1839
Cornell, George	1832–1845
Craft, John	1839
Cronk, Elijah	1832–1834
Davis, Samuel	1830–1833
Debevoise, George W.	1838–1841

Craftsman	Active date
Desmond, Daniel	1837
Eiselton, Henry	1820
Evans, Wilson	1837
Fagan, William	1836–1845
Fairbanks, Benjamin	1826–1830
Fairbanks, Samuel	1829–1830
Fealey, Thomas	1837–1839
Feeks, Joseph	1836–1841
Fox, Joseph	1822–1824
Fuller, Thomas	1838
Gilhooly, Andrew	1834–1835
Gilhooly & Son	1834–1835
Gilhooly, Thomas	1839–1860
Goadly, James	1833–1840
Goadly, Thomas	1839–1860
Goadly, William	1833–1849
Godfrey, Kemp	1828–1829
Hampton, Adam	1828–1860
Harris, Leonard	1829–1845
Havens, John F.	1834–1840
Hawley, William	1831–1840
Jabine, James	1831–1834
Jackson, Peter	1820–1821
Jackson, William	1832
Jackson, Wm. & Nathan	1820–1821
Johnston, Lewis	1832–1837
Jones, John H.	1833–1838
Kelley, James	1826–1836
Kerney, or Kearney, James J.	1836–1850
Kinzie, Kinsey, or Kensey, Thomas	1826–1843
Lamb, Owen L.	1833–1845
M'Avoy, John	1830–1841
M'Voy, John	1830–1841

Craftsman	Active date
Mallory, Daniel	1839–1841
Martin, Delaplane or Delaplaine	1838–1843
Mitchell, James	1835–1836
Mott, D.	1830
Mott & Holmes	1826–1829
Naylor & Winteringham	1828
Ockenden, James	1836–1843
Osborn, Thomas	1836
Picken, William	1830–1839
Rhoades, Edward	1835–1839
Robertson & Combs	1831
Scherf, Wolfgang	1837
Shaffer, John	1833–1834
Slocum, James	1831–1836
Smith, Francis	1828–1845
Stoddard, Francis	1833–1837
Tattersall, William	1840–1850
Teale, John	1835–1840
Thomas, T.	1835–1836
Thomas T. & A.	1837
Thomas, Thomas	1839–1841
Tucker & Horton	1839–1841
Tucker, Joseph	1843
Ward, Goadby & Co	1830–1843
Ward, Matthias	1833–1834
West, Bartholomew	1835
Whitehead, Isaac	1821–1841
Whitehead, Hawley	1817
Whitman, Nathaniel	1831–1837
Willard, William P.	1832–1835
William, William Jr.	1829–1834

FENDERS AND GRATES

A look at the catalogues of manufacturers who are producing fireplace equipment today indicates that they are trying to please all styles and tastes. There is a ready supply for those who want to produce a typical fireplace of the eighteenth century, with all its proper fittings. Manufacturers are also producing a hybrid type of Franklin stove which is better suited to the burning of coal than wood. They are also producing large basket grates in which wood or coal can be burned, and which are designed for use in a conventional fireplace. This plan is a compromise, but some people seem to want it. It all boils down as to whether the buyer wants a coal fire or a cracking wood fire in his fireplace. In America, a nostalgic feeling for the past can take any form the purchaser desires.

CHAPTER VI

A Gallery of Andirons

THE following is a portfolio of American andirons ranging from very early examples to very late ones. The first six examples are known as knife blade. Although they were made throughout the eighteenth century, they seem to have been most popular at mid-century.

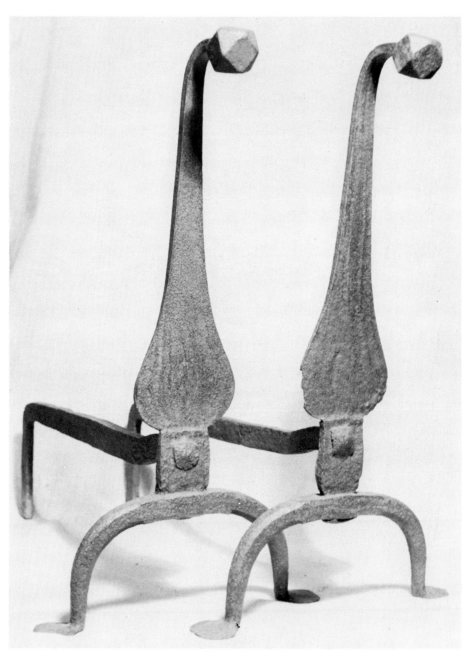

One of the earliest examples of knife blade andirons found in this survey, ca. 1750. There is ample evidence of forging in the shaping and construction of the andirons. The evident striations in the iron are caused by impurities. It is likely that at first the andirons were straight and later bent to fit into a smaller fireplace.

Kauffman Collection

Left, knife blade andirons with heads composed of diamond and flame finials. Note the lack of spiral grooves in the flame. Ca. 1750. *Right*, knife blade andirons with an unusual taper form in the shaft, ca. 1750.

Bowers Collection

Left, knife blade andirons lacking heads but with imprint "N. Starr" near the top of the shaft. Starr was a well-known arms manufacturer of Middletown, Connecticut. *Courtesy Ball and Ball*. *Right*, knife blade andirons with an attractive head composed of a diamond and flame. Penny feet are intact. Ca. 1750.

Bradley Antiques

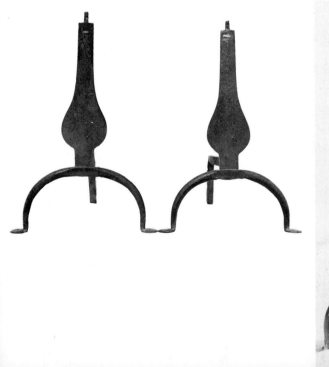
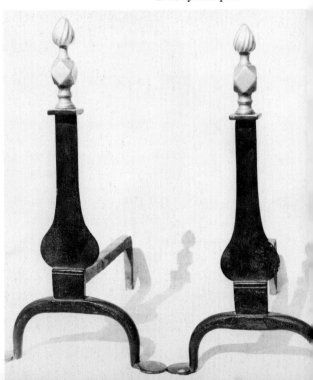

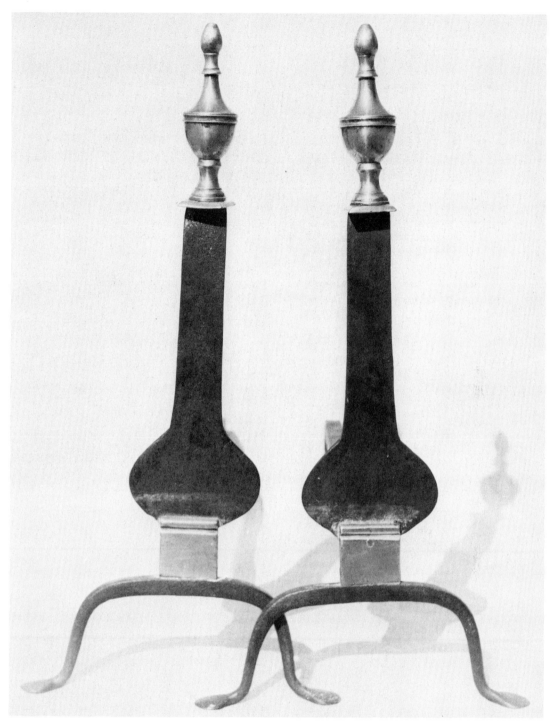

Knife blade andirons with curious enlarged shape just above the pedestal. Originally had two rows of beads on the urn. Ca. 1790.

Bradley Antiques

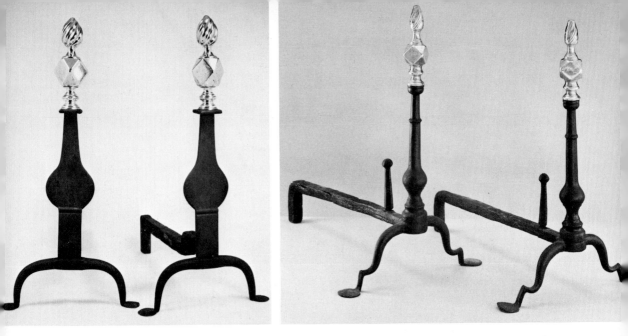

Left, unique example of knife blade andirons with unusually large pedestals, ca. 1750. *Bowers Collection*. *Right*, andirons of iron and brass with iron log stop, diamond and flame heads and penny feet, ca. 1750.

Courtesy Colonial Williamsburg

Left, brass andirons of the Chippendale period, ca. 1775. Height, twenty-six inches. *Right*, brass and cast iron andirons in the Queen Anne style, ca. 1750. Height, twenty-five inches.

Bowers Collection

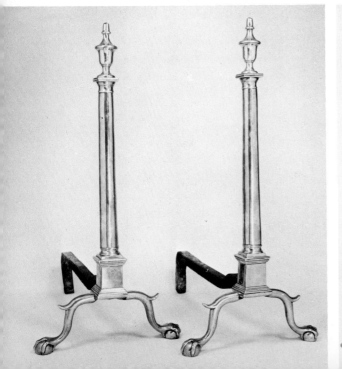

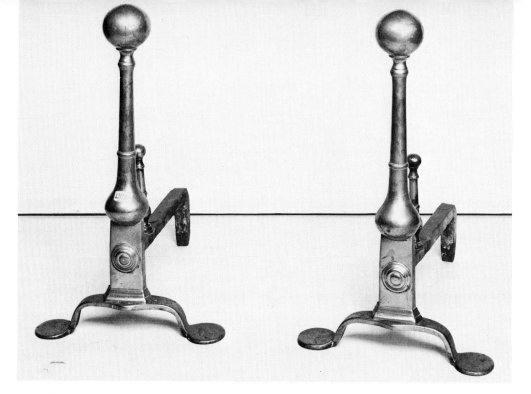

Brass andirons with low arched legs and penny feet. First half eighteenth century.

Kindig Antiques

Left, andirons of wrought iron, probably made in Pennsylvania in the mid-eighteenth century. *Courtesy Israel Sack Inc. Right,* brass andirons of the late eighteenth century. A combination of details (Federal urn with ball-and-claw feet) is not an uncommon feature in the pattern of many andirons.

Bowers Collection

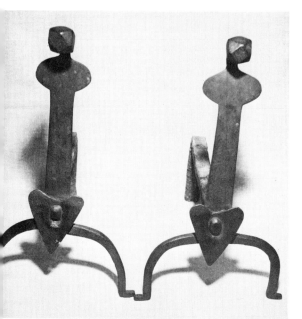

 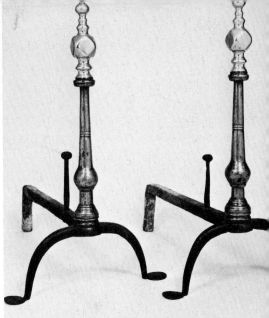

Left, a pair of andirons with urn heads but penny feet. *Right*, an attractive pair of andirons of wrought iron and brass with diamond heads and spool-like finials. Second quarter of the eighteenth century.

Bowers Collection

Left, andirons of cast iron with large pedestals and sharply tapering shafts. Mid-eighteenth century. *Right*, an elegant pair of andirons. Notice the log stops are replicas of the front columns including the pedestals.

Bowers Collection

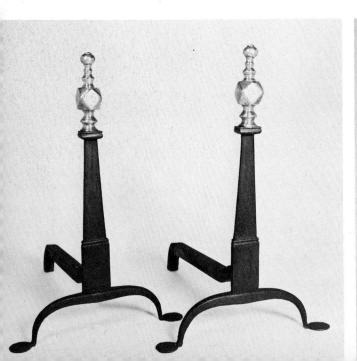 

Left, wrought iron and brass andirons of the late seventeenth or early eighteenth century. The iron work was not as skillfully done on these as on later examples. *Bowers Collection*. *Right*, andirons of wrought iron showing considerable evidence of deterioration. Thousands of small examples like this one were made to be used in chamber fireplaces in the eighteenth century.

Left, trestle-footed andirons of cast iron with cast brass finials. *Right*, steel andirons with iron billet bars. Probably British. c. 1750.

Courtesy Colonial Williamsburg

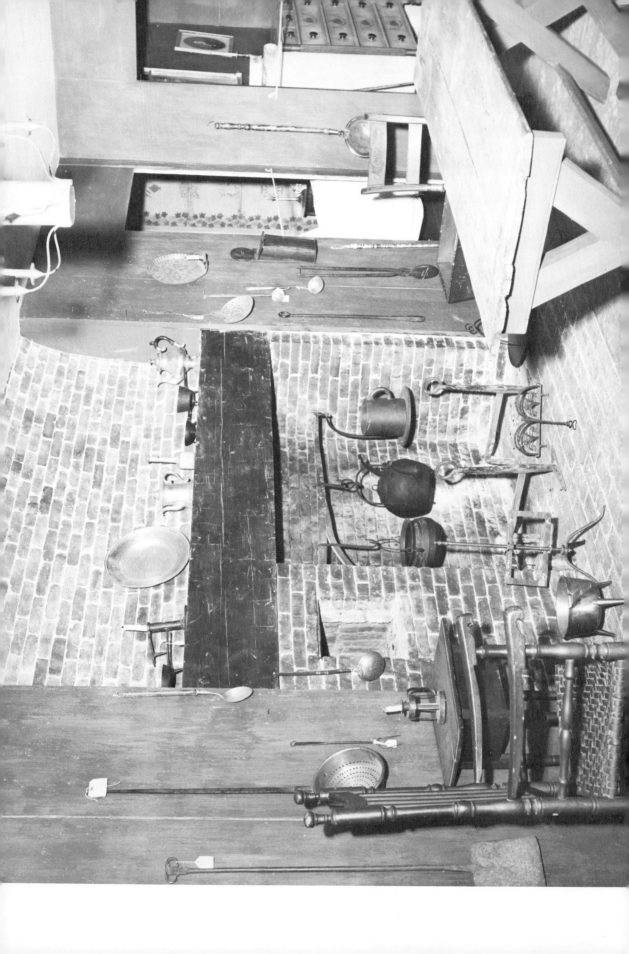

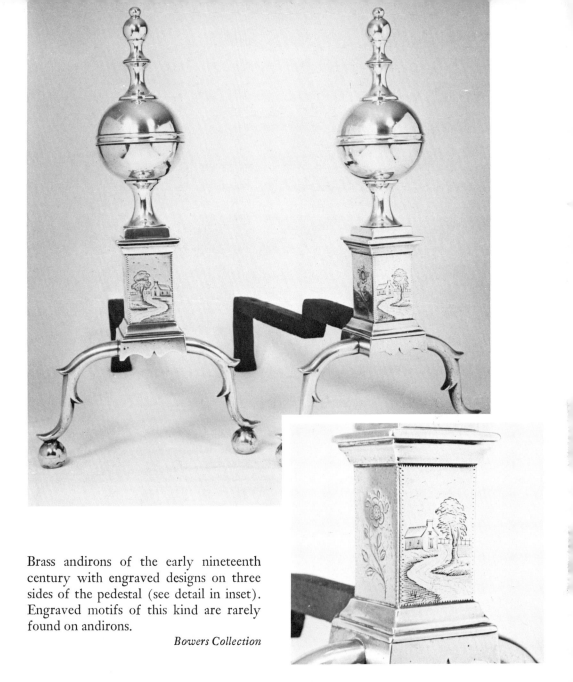

Brass andirons of the early nineteenth century with engraved designs on three sides of the pedestal (see detail in inset). Engraved motifs of this kind are rarely found on andirons.

Bowers Collection

All iron trestle-footed andiron in the kitchen fireplace of the Stencil House at Shelburne Museum, Shelburne, Vermont.

Courtesy Shelburne Museum

Brass andirons with particularly attractive spurs on the legs. Probably made in Philadelphia in the last decade of the eighteenth century.

Courtesy Colonial Williamsburg

A virtually unique pair of miniature brass andirons 5¾ inches tall. Their pattern obviously matches the full-sized ball and steeple andiron. The pedestal was made in two halves (see detail right). Probably very late eighteenth or early nineteenth century.

Courtesy Mr. and Mrs. H. L. Chalfant

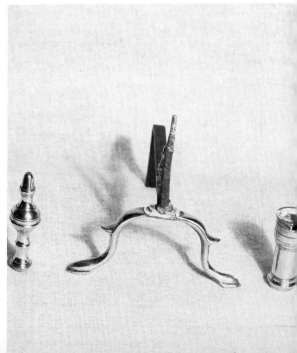

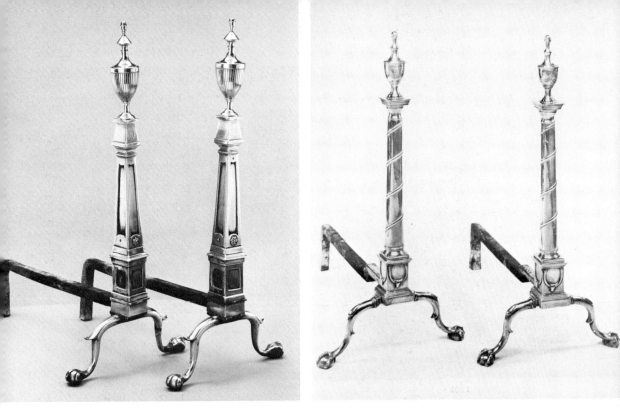

Left, andirons with columns fabricated of sheet brass. Iron billet bars. Made in the United States, ca. 1790. *Courtesy Colonial Williamsburg. Right*, an unusual pair of andirons with several outstanding features. Among these are the shell pattern on the knees, the engraved spiral vine encircling the shafts, the antler motif applied to the pedestal, and the engraved urns of the heads. At one time, they had gadrooned moldings at the base of the plinth, now lost.
Courtesy David Worcester Place

Andirons of cast iron advertised on the trade card of Brackett and Joseph Webb of Boston. The card was engraved by Paul Revere.
Courtesy J. P. Remensnyder

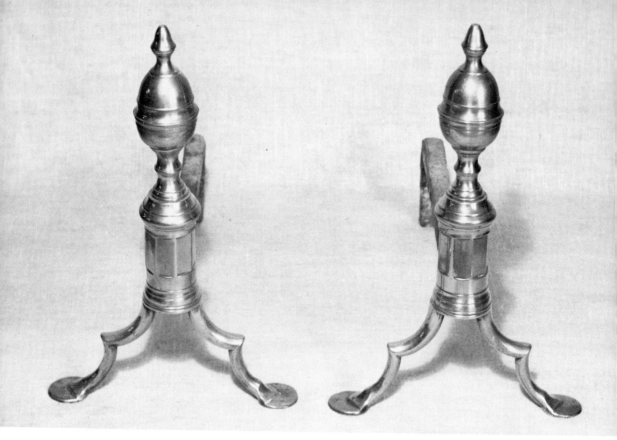

An attractive low pair of brass andirons with octagonal pedestals and penny feet. Probably made at the turn of the nineteenth century.

Courtesy Bradley Antiques

Andirons made by John Molineux of Boston, last decade of the eighteenth century. His name and Boston are evident on the brass plate between the column and the log stop. Height, 14½ inches.

Bowers Collection

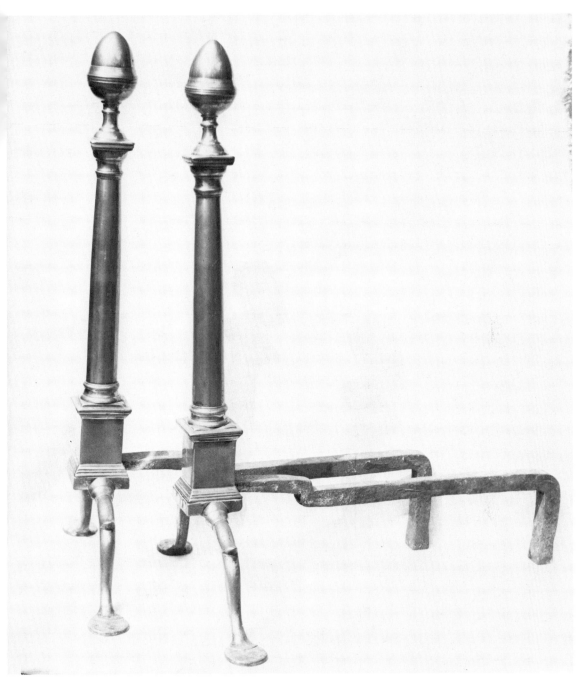

Brass andirons with acorn heads and penny feet. These feet were used simultaneously with the claw-and-ball style.

Kauffman Collection

An unsigned pair of brass andirons probably made very early in the nineteenth century. The escalloped plinth is reminiscent of the late eighteenth century.

Courtesy Bradley Antiques

Low type brass andirons of the late eighteenth century, lemon or acorn head.

Bowers Collection

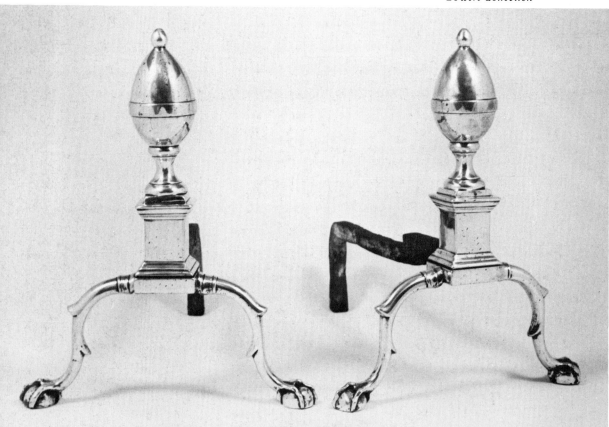

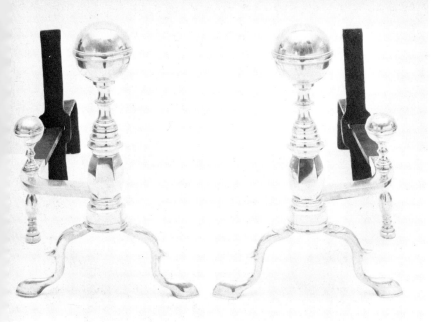 

A signed pair of brass andirons made by the William C. Hunneman family early in the nineteenth century. The family name and city are stamped on a brass plate covering the top of the billet bar between the log stop and the main shaft (see inset). Very few examples of this style are known bearing the Hunneman imprint.

Courtesy Henry Francis DuPont Winterthur Museum

Decorated andirons of wrought iron. The tracery design on the front of the column was probably done with a cold chisel. The holes near the top of the columns were possibly for holding spit hooks on the back side. Early eighteenth century.

Courtesy Henry Francis DuPont Winterthur Museum

One of a pair of handsome brass andirons with engraved designs on the pedestal and the head. The log stop is not quite in the same style. Ca. 1800.
Courtesy Philip Cowan

Brass andirons by R. Whittingham of New York City, last decade of the eighteenth or early nineteenth century. An urn and a weeping willow tree are engraved on the front side of the pedestal.

Brass andirons with acorn head, smooth shaft, cabriole legs, and ball-and-claw feet. Probably made in Philadelphia in the late eighteenth century. Height, twenty-six inches.

Bowers Collection

Left, a very rare pair of brass andirons made and signed by William Holmes Webb, who worked in Warren, Maine, about 1800. The name is stamped in a circle around the log stop on the brass plate covering the front end of the billet bar. *Right*, brass andirons marked "B. Edmands." Edmands worked in Charlestown, Mass., ca. 1800. Marked examples of his work are scarce.

Bowers Collection

Left, brass andirons marked "Iohn Molineux" on top side of the billet bar. Later examples by the same man are marked "John Molineux." Ca. 1800. *Bowers Collection*. *Right*, brass andirons with a reeded edge on the vase form of the head. Probably made in Philadelphia, ca. 1810.

Kauffman Collection

CHAPTER VII

Men of the Craft

THERE are various ways to round out the picture and get a true perspective of American fireplace furnishings. One of the most logical, and certainly the easiest, is to examine surviving examples. This procedure tells much about the workmanship of craftsmen; it reveals the efficacy of design in the objects, and frequently indicates the manner in which these fittings have withstood "wear and tear" over the years. This is largely an impersonal appraisal, but one has learned something of the maker such as his honesty in workmanship and the use of materials, or whether he has taken shortcuts to cheat the purchaser, or if his products are "all wool and a yard wide."

There was certainly little high drama connected with the making of fireplace fittings, and, in fact, little documented material relating to it has survived. We know of some makers only because of a record in the form of an inventory (made usually at death), as in the case of Henry Shrimpton. From it can be inferred a tale of "rags to riches," a theme that has always been popular with the residents of the New World. That is the substance of much of the fabric of which it was made. The story of Jonathan Jackson can also be gathered from an inventory, to which some important press notices can be added. In the case of John Bailey, both press notices and surviving artifacts remain to tell his story. As for the Whittinghams, only their artifacts together with the bare records found in business directories have survived.

An examination of these resources reveals a story that begins with the pioneer life of Henry Shrimpton in mid-seventeenth century Boston, and ends with the Whittinghams who worked in New York City at the turn of the eighteenth century. All told, these men are outstanding examples of American success in business and technology. Shrimpton and Jackson were doubtless outstanding craftsmen, but are remembered chiefly because they became wealthy in a society where wealth was an uncommon achievement. Bailey was a jack-of-all-trades, and the Whittinghams were master craftsmen. A niche for each is reserved in this survey of personalities of the trade.

HENRY SHRIMPTON

The man who attracts notice first is Henry Shrimpton, born about the year 1615 in Bednall Green, England. He came to live in Boston about 1639, and in that year at a selectmen's meeting was granted permission to follow the trade of "brayser" and be an inhabitant of the town.

Before scrutinizing the extensive inventory of his possessions, drawn up at his death in 1666, some attempt should be made to further describe his trade. *The Oxford Universal Dictionary* defines a brazier as one who works in brass. The term is more specifically (and precisely) defined in *A Supplement to Chamber's Cyclopedia: or Universal Dictionary of Arts and Sciences,* Vol. I, London, 1753, as follows:

> BRAZIER, an artificer who makes and sells pans, pots, kettles, and other kitchen utensils, and brass ware. . . . The implements used by a brazier are a forge, wherein they burn charcoal to heat their work, a twibil, wherewith to hold their work, divers sorts of anvils and hammers, wherewith to beat; also pans, ladles, sheers, borax box, a lath (lathe) for turning, etc.

Unfortunately, it is impossible to determine which items in the Shrimpton inventory were made by him. If he had made andirons, he would have been technically known as a founder. A brazier made objects of sheet brass, as the Chambers definition indicates, while a founder made objects of cast brass. The available evidence suggests that he was a brazier and a founder, a very uncommon combination of crafts at any time. The listing in his inventory is "Working tools for pewter and brass" at a value of £67–00–00. There does not seem to be any question about his activity in making objects of pewter; however, no surviving examples of his work in either metal is known to the collecting fraternity today. There is a profusion of objects of both metals in the inventory.

It is also evident that he was, at his death, a merchant, for his inventory includes some merchandise which he would not have made as a craftsman in metals. His stock included many textiles, furs, iron, rum, molasses, etc. This change in vocation was a natural one in the seventeenth and eighteenth centuries. A man began his adult life as a craftsman, but as he became better known and more prosperous, he employed men to work in his back shop, while he moved to the front where his merchandise was sold. Later, he often expanded his business to include products of others, who were not associated with him, and imports as well. The early rise of the industrial revolution in England made manufactured items available from abroad which were not easily produced here.

It is also evident that he operated a production shop until his death, for it has been pointed out, tools were listed in his inventory. It also should be noted that his huge stores of unwrought and scrap (shruff) copper and brass were possibly the results of barter rather than intended supplies for his shop. Some of this scrap metal might have been for resale to other craftsmen of the town. It is plainly evident, therefore, that Shrimpton operated a workshop and a department store, in today's terminology. Among the items of the inventory one finds:

60 pc. old armor	03–00–00
6 gal. rum	00–10–00
2,000 ft. plank and boards	06–00–00
? copper bars at 12 sh.	11–04–00
100 barrels of tar	40–00–00
5 hoghs. French salt	05–00–00
1 barrel powder (gun)	09–00–00
90 bu. Indian corn at 2:6	10–00–00
42 barrels pork	126–00–00
19 tankards at 3 : 10	03–12–00
20 caudle cups at 3 : 4	03–06–00
5 gross large alkamy spoons	15–00–00
6 large upright Chambor potts	10–00–00

A close examination of the Shrimpton inventory reveals that at least a few of the Puritans must have been living in real luxury by the middle of the seventeenth century. They seem to have had plenty of wine and rum (used mostly at funerals) and a variety of household items beyond belief. The really ponderable entries for this survey, however, are the brass andirons Shrimpton had in his home and his store.

It has formerly been concluded by experts, and in this study as well, that andirons used in America in the seventeenth century were of cast iron or wrought iron with "knobs" (finials) of brass. Now the researcher is faced with the fact that as early as 1666, brass andirons were used in the fireplaces of Boston. Shrimpton not only used them, he sold them.

This account does not suggest that one or two scattered examples were found in Boston, but that many were in daily use. The question demanding an answer is, were they made here, or were they made abroad? It might be noted that other items in the inventory were made of cast brass. Some brass candlesticks (could have been fabricated of sheet, but doubtful), mortars, etc., suggest casting in brass, but the real question is the origin and style of the brass andirons.

The nearest help that can be found concerning brass andirons of the period is in examples known to have existed in England. The following excerpt from the *English Fireplace and Its Accessories* by L. A. Shuffrey throws some light on the problem:

> Haddon Hall, Derbyshire, fortunately retains many of its fireplaces in the original condition; that in the state bedroom, shown in Plate LIX has andirons, the lower parts of which are wrought iron, almost identical in design with the Henry VIII pair at Knole, surmounted by cast brass standards of baluster form. Brass balusters may be seen again in the Long Gallery, but of heavier and less graceful form, the supports being of cast brass formed of arched legs and heads of animals, with the head at the intersection with the billet bar. In both cases these stand on a slightly raised stone hearth, and in the latter there is a front hearth of marble arranged in octagons and squares. This same treatment is met with again in the handsome pair of bronze andirons in Moyns Park, Essex, popularly supposed to have been cast from guns taken from

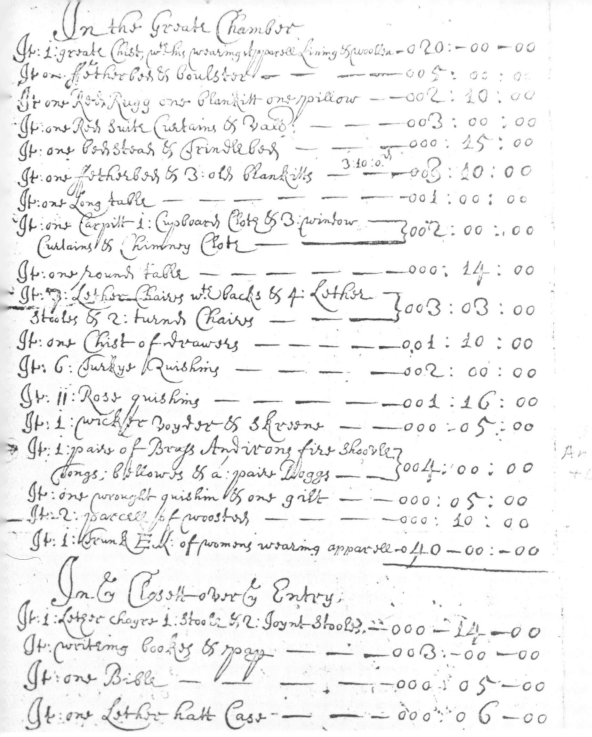

In the Greate Chamber

It: 1 greate Chist, w:th his wearing Apparell Lining & woollen	020 : 00 – 00
It: one ffetherbed & boulster	005 : 00 : 00
It: one Redd Rugg one blankitt one pillow	002 : 10 : 00
It: one Redd Suite Curtains & Vailes	003 : 00 : 00
It: one bedsteade & Trindlebed	000 : 15 : 00
It: one fetherbed & 3: old blankitts 3:10:0.	003 : 10 : 00
It: one Long table	001 : 00 : 00
It: one Carpitt 1: Cupboard Cloth & 3: window Curtains & Chimney Cloth	002 : 00 : 00
It: one round table	000 : 14 : 00
It: 3: Lether Chaires w:th backs & 4: Lether Stooles & 2: turnd Chaires	003 : 03 : 00
It: one Chist of drawers	001 : 10 : 00
It: 6: Turkye Cuishins	002 : 00 : 00
It: 11: Rose cuishins	001 : 16 : 00
It: 1: wicker boyder & 3 shevens	000 : 05 : 00
It: 1: paire of Brass Andirons fire shoovle Tongs, bellowes & a: paire Doggs	004 : 00 : 00
It: one wrought cuishim & one gilt	000 : 05 : 00
It: 2: parcell of woosters	000 : 10 : 00
It: 1: Trunk full of womens wearing apparell	040 – 00 : – 00

In ye Closett over ye Entry:

It: 1: Lether chayre 1: Stoole & 2: Joynt Stooles	000 – 14 – 00
It: writing bookes & pay	003 : – 00 – 00
It: one Bible	000 : 05 – 00
It: one Lether hatt Case	000 : 06 – 00

Part of Page One of the inventory of Henry Shrimpton. The objects "In the Greate Chamber" are listed including one "paire of Brass Andirons, fire shoovle, Tongs, bellows, and a paire doggs."

Courtesy Suffolk County Probate Court, Boston, Mass.

Brass andirons with iron legs of the seventeenth century. Shrimpton's andirons may have resembled these.

Courtesy Colonial Williamsburg

the Spanish Armada (1588). These are 4 ft. 6 in. high and 2 ft. wide at the base, and the workmanship is both vigorous and refined.

Thus, it is evident that baluster type brass andirons with wrought iron bases could have been listed in the Shrimpton inventory. A few examples are known in America which could in some respects fit the description from Shuffrey, and they have been regarded as English or Dutch in origin. They may have been some of the andirons in the Shrimpton inventory.

In conclusion, it should be mentioned that regardless of the style and material of the andirons in his inventory, Shrimpton was a prosperous man. In his personal inventory and in his home was found gold worth £25, English money £121, pieces of eight £46, New England money £493, plus items such as two gold rings, one silver box, 13 pair of shoes, 3 pair of boots, 2 pair of spurs, one old saddle and furniture, 1 pair of pistols, and a quantity of mace and cinnamon. The total value of the contents of the closet was £751. In the great chamber, he had rugs, blankets, pillows, a cupboard, curtains, a long table, a chimney cloth, and brass andirons. The total value of his estate was £12,000 in round numbers. Ledlie Laughlin states in *Pewter in America* that he was the second wealthiest pewterer known to have lived in America.

But this man cannot be appraised alone on the wealth he accumulated. He could have had all his money hid in the floor of his house, and lived on the bare necessities of life. There is ample evidence that he lived the life of a cultured gentleman of the era. As a matter of fact, any man who had 13 pair of shoes might almost be accused of "high living" in those days of bleak austerity. He had curtains all over the house, and in each room he had a pair of brass andirons, except in the kitchen where he had fire irons, a jack, 2 spits, shovel & tongs, and one pair of bellows. And to top it all, in the entry hall, he had a fowling piece and a mirror. The andiron collecting fraternity can be very happy to number Shrimpton as a member.

JONATHAN JACKSON

Another early craftsman who probably made furnishings for the fireplace is Jonathan Jackson. He was born in Boston, on December 28, 1672. No claim of "rags to riches" can be made for this man, because he was one of a second generation of Jacksons born in America, with a substantial background as far as worldly goods are concerned. His grandfather, Edward Jackson, was the immigrant. An excerpt from *Three Hundred Years American* by Alice and Bettina Jackson tells of his holdings.

> In all directions stretched Edward Jackson's lands, partly bounded by the Charles River and the highway. Eventually his holdings amounted to some sixteen hundred acres, including the pieces called "Bushes Meadow" Baulding Pate Hill and meadow land, a pine forest with long marsh and upland, a cedar swamp with adjoining uplands and other parcels.
>
> According to Edward's long and careful inventory, his spacious mansion contained more than the usual amount of furniture for his day, hangings, floor coverings, tableware, and kitchen utensils. On the first floor, were the Great Parlor, Southern Parlor, Southwest Parlor, Kitchen and Back Room. But most important was the large Central Hall with its fireplace. Upstairs were the West Chamber, the Southwest Chamber, in which Edward kept his library, a room for spinning and weaving, and, of course, the Garrett. . . .
>
> As well-to-do farmers, the Jackson family lived in substantial comfort, far more so than many other early New England colonists.

In the account just quoted, there is an inventory of the furnishings of the important rooms and also an extensive accounting of fruits, grains, and livestock, usually considered very important to any farmer. Lest one become overimpressed with the heritage of a member of the Jackson family, one must be reminded that in those days many families had as many as twelve to fifteen children, and one is mentioned with twenty future heirs.

Despite the division of the estate into many parts, it is evident the Jacksons were good stewards of their heritage. Jonathan left the farm. He seems to have become an entrepreneur early in life for "On January 9, 1699 Jonathan Jackson and John Dolbeare bought jointly from John Wiswall wharves and real estate near the Town Dock, and there, whether in one or separate shops, conducted their braziery and pewter-making business." It should be parenthetically noted here that very few pieces of pewter have been identified as the product of Dolbeare, while none have been found that can be attributed to Jackson. It should be noted also that Jackson was identified as a brazier in the inventory of his estate in 1736. However, in his inventory is listed a "Sett Pewterers Tools" valued at £33 11s. and over 1500 pounds of "Pewter Moulds."

The inventory (consisting of twenty pages) is divided into three sections: 1. Goods of English Manufacture, 2. Goods of New England Manufacture, and 3. Household Furnishings and Real Estate.

Jackson obviously followed the same business route as Shrimpton, although it is really not known definitely that either man, Shrimpton or Jackson, left his workshop to sell merchandise in the store. The comprehensive inventory does include many items that cannot be considered as products of a brazier; consequently, there is little doubt that Jackson became a merchant. Another argument in favor of his having left the shop is the fact that no product can be identified as that of Mr. Jackson. This theory does have its alternative, for, even if he had no part in actual production, it is likely that the products made in his shop would have his name imprinted on all finished products.

The "Goods of English Manufacture" are of secondary interest in this survey; however, they did include a number of items of importance as far as fireplace furnishings are concerned. Many were made of iron, which indicates that the local products of brass and pewter were possibly products of Jackson, the brazier, and Dolbeare, the pewterer. Among the items listed are the following: coffin handles, dishes, compasses, candlesticks, chaffin dishes, fire steels, box iron frames, gim bletts, nails, spikes, fishhooks, brass desk hunges, hatchets, H hinges, chest hinges, cocks, trunk locks, padlocks, thumb latches, closet locks, iron ladles, stock locks, needles, shoe pinches, wood (handle) warming pans, wood screws, English steel, sheer steel, spelter, sheep sheers, staples, bedscrews, mouse traps, jacks (smoke jacks), tongs and shovels, tacks, and bell metal skillets. No pewter is included, so logically it might be assumed that the pewter found in the inventory was locally produced. It is important to notice that warming pans had handles of wood as early as 1736; however, iron handles continued to be used for they are listed among the products of New England manufacture. This is one specific example that the avant-garde in style was coming from Europe.

Among the items of New England manufacture are found the following: 24 cast dogs with brass heads, wrot dogs, old brass bars, copper funnels, nail hammers, hooks and hinges, casement hinges, iron warming pan handles, warming pan joints (hinges), brass knockers, brass skillets, brass ladles, thumb latches, fish leds, cod lines, five foot grindstones, hasps and staples, chamber pots, old pewter, bloodporringers, hard metal plates, paper, sledges, hammers and stakes, large cannon balls, trowells, tankards, copper tacks, twine, frying pans, wine potts, brass skails, sockets for warming pans, sauce pans, tongs, shovels, pewterer's tools (at 33–11–00) and brass tools (at 32–05–04). Thereafter follow two pages of "wares" described as defective, which would be called "seconds" today. They have no particular bearing on this survey. It is very unusual, however, for merchandise of such quality to be listed, as it usually was discarded as worthless. Of course, it may have been destined for that end in this case.

The problem of the moment, of course, is to try to determine what Jackson and Dolbeare made and sold. The fact that some pewter objects bearing a Dolbeare imprint are known today suggests that he was the pewterer. And it might be said that they are very outstanding pieces. If that is the case, then the work of Jackson the brazier would explain the presence of objects such as warming pans, sauce pans, brass skails, brass skillets, brass ladles, etc. It should be particularly noted that he made not only warming pans but also some of the appendages such as sockets and hinges, which he obviously sold to men who knew how to make only pans. His stock of both iron and wooden handles indicates that the 1736 period was one of transition from iron to wood. It cannot be determined if he made any of the handles which he sold, as none were made of brass. It seems rather evident that he, like Shrimpton, was a craftsman-merchant, who sold items he did not make when there was a demand for them.

The objects in the inventory relevant to this survey are the andirons, namely, 24 cast dogs, brass head dogs, and wrot dogs. The presence of objects of cast brass articles such as brass knockers and brass head dogs suggests that Jackson was not only a brazier but was also a founder. The position toward Jackson being a founder is strongly supported by the advertisement his wife Mary inserted in the *Boston Gazette*, Oct. 4, 1736, only four months after the date of the inventory in which she clearly advertises "Founders Ware," including andirons. The loose use of the trade terminology is evident from the heading of her advertisement, "Brazier's Wares."

> BRAZIERS' WARES.—Mary Jackson, at the Brazen-Head in Cornhill, makes and sells all sorts of Brass and Founders Ware, as Hearths, Fenders, Shovels, and Tongs, Hand-irons, Candlesticks, Brasses for Chaises and Saddles, of the newest fashion; all sorts of Mill Brasses, Mortars, Cocks, large and small; all sorts of polished Brazier's Ware, at reasonable rates. A Quantity of Large brown Paper fit for sheathing ships, to be sold: Likewise buys old Copper, Brass, Pewter, Lead, and Iron.

In summary, it is probable that Henry Shrimpton was making brass andirons in the mid-seventeenth century, and Jonathan Jackson was making them in and before 1736. It is not likely that his wife would have struck out on her own with such an important new item as brass andirons, if they had not been made previously by her husband. It is also likely that her foundry cast only objects of brass, those cast of iron being bought for resale from another craftsman of the region. The inventory specifically states that Jonathan sold cast iron mortars. It is also probable that the "wrot" andirons were made of iron and were bought from another craftsman who specialized in fashioning objects of wrought iron. None of the items in Mary Jackson's advertisement suggests the production of iron objects in her husband's shop.

It also might be parenthetically pointed out that two entries of "blood porringers" appear in the Jackson inventory. There have been rumors of porringers being used for surgical bleeding practices, but this is the first time such evidence has been seen by the authors.

The expeditious insertion of a notice in the public press four months after her husband's death indicates that Mary Jackson was an aggressive businesswoman. Presumably, one of her sons had been trained as a brazier and/or founder, for a considerable number of items of sheet and cast brass appear in a later advertisement. Another evidence of her business acumen can be found in an advertisement she placed in the *Boston Gazette* Sept. 27/Oct. 4, 1736.

Assayer.—If any persons desire to know the true value of ores, minerals, or metals, of what kind soever, they may have them justly assay'd on reasonable terms, by Robt Baden, at Mrs. Mary Jackson's Foundry, at the Brazen Head in Cornhill, Boston.

It is evident that the constant search for metals by many of the colonists created enough demand for this service to warrant her hiring a skilled assayer. Such a procedure would have been a logical one. The absence of references to objects of pewter in her advertisement of Sept. 27/Oct. 4 suggests that at that time, if not earlier, John Dolbeare did not have a working interest in the business. Whether partnership had been dissolved prior to Jackson's death, or whether, at his death, Mrs. Jackson had bought out Dolbeare's interest is unknown. At any rate, the "company" molds were part of the inventory at Jackson's death.

Mary Jackson was a persistent advertiser, for on May 15, 1760, she placed a very lengthy notice in the *Boston News-Letter* under the company name Mary Jackson and Son with no mention of the assay service she had previously advertised.

The fact that Mary Jackson opened a new shop is further evidence that she must have been a "natural" as far as business management was concerned. This is the first mention of her son; it is not known exactly when he became a member of the business. The advertisement continues to carry entries such as andirons, fire tools, fenders, fire pans, and other items previously mentioned. In addition, she was carrying a large line of London pewter, including teapots (fantastic in 1760), and she also stocked porringers. The rarity of English porringers and teapots of the mid-eighteenth century in museums and other collections today makes their appearance in America as early as 1760 noteworthy. She also advertised London glew, London combs, ivory and horn, Dutch spectacles, brass and iron thimbles and a great variety of London, Birmingham & Sheffield cutlery. One hundred and forty entries appear in the advertisement. The first paragraph of the advertisement is as follows:

> Braziers' Ware.—Mary Jackson and Son, have opened their shop, since the late fire, a few doors from the Court House, opposite Deacon Phillip's in Cornhill; where their customers may be supply'd with the following articles, Viz:—

Although it is only of academic interest here, a hasty glance at Jackson's household inventory will suggest the quality of his furnishings, as appraised at his death. A partial listing includes: 1 japanned tea table & board, 12 cain chairs, glass sconces with arms, 1 glass lantern, 1 large black walnut table, 12 china cups and saucers, 106 oz. of wrought plate (silver), tobacco tongs, bellows, many shovels and tongs, delph plates, 1 oval table, 1 clock, 6 leather chairs, kitchen table and linen towling, calico curtains, 10 table cloths, 12 pillow cases, a silk bed quilt, 1 feather bed bolster and sheet, several looking glasses, hollans sheets, 2 doz. napkins, chest of drawers, rugs, and many other objects of similar nature.

Ledlie Laughlin states in *Pewter in America* that:

> "he (Jonathan Jackson) died May 4, 1736, perhaps the wealthiest of all American pewterers, leaving an estate of over £30,00.

It is difficult to truly appraise the stature of Jonathan Jackson in the area of fireplace furnishings. As a brazier and a merchant, it is evident that thousands of ordinary household objects such as pans, pots, trivets, warming pans, etc., were made by him or sold in his store. His wealth combined with the richness of his household furnishings indicate that he was one of the most discriminating men of his era. He was engaged in civic activities as well as being a member of the First Church. Of equal interest to his activities are those of his wife. Few, if any, women of the time headed a business as large and aggressive as hers. It would be an interesting experience to explore the status of the business at her death.

JOHN BAILEY

At this point, it is evident to the reader that information about the men who produced fireplace furnishings in Colonial America is very scarce. The two inventories examined so far have been unusually useful in evaluating the contributions of Henry Shrimpton and Jonathan Jackson; however, the fact that there are no signed objects by either man is unfortunate. Although no inventory is available for John Bailey, data about him has been obtained from other sources, and, fortunately, some of his signed products are known to exist today.

Bailey has been previously described as a jack-of-all-trades, and herewith is the evidence for such a designation. On March 4, 1771, Bailey and Youle placed the following advertisement in the *New York Gazeteer* and *The Weekly Mercury:*

> BAILEY & YOULE, Cutlers from Sheffield at their shop Near the Merchants Coffee-House, Makes all sorts of surgeon instruments, trusses, steel collars for children, irons for lame legs, and silversmiths tools; likewise grinds all sorts of knives, razors, shears, and scissors, to look as neat as when new: also fixes new plades into any kind of hafts, cut gentlemen and ladies names, with numbers for numbering linen and books, wherewith they give either red or black ink which will not wash out, and may be used by any person without trouble or inconveniency.
>
> They likewise have for sale Silk stockings, silver hafted knives, and forks, ivory and ebony ditto, redwood, plain and silver ferrel'd ditto, stag, buck and bone ditto, carving knives and forks, penknives of all sorts, bones and razor straps, razors of all sorts, fine cast steel scissors, common ditto, taylors shears and thimbles, tortoise shell combs, and common butcher knives, saws, steeles and cleavers, shoemakers knives of all sorts, coffee gaffs, netting and knitting needles, sword canes with cocks, plain ditto, double and single plane irons, carving gouges and chissels, watch crystals and silver buckles, of the newest fashion. N. B. They give the greatest price for old gold, and silver lace, and old gold and silver.

This advertisement is an unusual document furnishing valuable information about Bailey and his business associate. It should be mentioned immediately that it is headed by a drawing illustrating some of the items enumerated in the advertisement. Also, on a panel below the illustrated items is the statement, set apart from the body of the text, that Bailey and Youle were cutlers from Sheffield. This fact is of significance. Sheffield for many years had been known as the "capital" of the cutlery trade. This was by far the best recommendation they could have mentioned at that time. It implied that they had served at least seven years as apprentices to a master cutler, and that they had left Sheffield to explore the business potential of the New World, specifically New York, for then it was a rapidly growing metropolis, and prospects for trade were good.

The illustration above their name is perhaps the most unusual feature of the advertisement. It consists of line drawings of pistol handled knives and forks, the forks having two tines, a pair of scissors, a bleeding knife, a razor, pen knife, sword and a few other objects which cannot be identified. The knife and fork are of particular interest for they are evidence that such sophisticated objects were in daily use at that time, generally, however, by the upper classes. The middle classes got along with less costly utensils. It should be noted that those illustrated are very graceful in form, establishing Bailey and Youle as discriminating craftsmen and merchants. At least Bailey is known to have been also a silversmith. The sword is of great interest because one of Bailey's products was carried by Washington in the Revolutionary War.

The verbal contents of the advertisement definitely stamp Bailey as a cutler by virtue of the item "surgeons" instruments. It is difficult to determine if Bailey or Youle made any specific items, but both apparently were cutlers and their capabilities in many ways must have been similar. Bailey's talents will become more evident as the survey continues.

Doubtless the most interesting item in the advertisement, other than cutlery, is "steel collars for children." The writer has read of other colonial craftsmen who made a similar product. The inhumanity of such a device is very startling today. One can ponder over the response of Bailey's contemporaries to the making of such an article. Was it used on the streets or only in the home? Was it padded with soft felt or leather, or did the child grow callouses where the collar rubbed his neck? Was it universally used for children, or did only the most recalcitrant become its victims? What did it cost? Were there sizes for big necks and little necks? Could a neighbor borrow one for a day or two? Certainly, these questions will never be answered but one must wonder what kind of a man made "steel collars for children."

Maybe the inhumanity of steel collars was balanced out by the fact that he made "irons for lame legs." All told, it was an interesting business. One is quite surprised to find "irons for lame legs," for presumably they are a modern device and appear to be the product of modern technology. Presumably, they were made of iron or steel, steel being less likely to bend. One might also wonder if they were as costly then as they are today, as well as how efficient they were in relieving the patient's malady. Of course, many men made trusses, and strange as it may seem, out of metal.

Most of the above are the natural products of a cutler; however, the cutting of "gentlemens and ladies names, with numbers for linen" seems to be a skill of the engraver rather than the cutler. Of course, it might be taken for granted that a competent cutler and silversmith could engrave satisfactorily. It is also interesting that indelible ink for the numbering procedure was available at that time.

The next advertisement found in this survey indicates that Bailey struck out in business on his own. This venture was the result of his moving to Fishkill, New York (some distance north along the Hudson River). One can only surmise that Youle stayed in New York to continue his trade. There certainly was no mention of his moving with Bailey. The following advertisement appeared in the *New York Packet*, and *The American Advertiser*, on May 14, 1778.

> John Bailey, Cutler from New York, is removed from Fredricksburg to Fish-Kill, where he intends to carry on his business extensively in its several branches. Workmen are wanted, such as

Cutlers, Capable of making Surgeons instruments, who can file well, Silversmiths, White and Blacksmiths, who will meet with the best encouragement.

Bailey's move to Fishkill was motivated by the fact that the British occupied New York City, while large sections of the American army were stationed at Fishkill. Fishkill had consisted of about fifty houses in the space of two miles. There the army placed its magazines, hospitals, workshops, etc., all of which formed an encampment larger than the original town site. The soldiers built barracks of logs, and the Van Wyck mansion was the officers' headquarters, presumably, often visited by Washington, Lafayette, Von Steuben, Putman, etc. It was here that Bailey probably contracted to make the silver hilted sword which Washington carried.

At Fishkill, Bailey was obviously engaged in the production of war material, and he was obviously advertising in New York for craftsmen to follow him there. His need for silversmiths indicates that a substantial amount of work would be available for such craftsmen, although Bailey is thought to have personally made Washington's sword, since it was signed, J. Bailey, Fishkill. The blacksmiths were needed to forge the sword blades, and the whitesmiths to finish them "bright" or white. Bailey apparently returned to New York soon after the war, and in 1785 he was paid ten pounds for "iron work" which he did for the New York Common Council.

John Bailey's silver hilted sword worn by George Washington through most of the Revolution. Its identity is established by its appearance in the portrait of Washington begun by Peale at Valley Forge in 1778.

Courtesy Smithsonian Institution

By 1790, Bailey had become engaged in another trade, namely, the founding of objects of brass. This information has been culled from a billhead dated New York, November 5, 1790, on which is illustrated a knife box, candlestick, (undoubtedly brass), an andiron, a teakettle (possibly brass), a fire shovel, and a fender. The entry on the billhead is, "To Pr. of Endirons £5–5–0." The printed heading indicates that Bailey was then a brassfounder, coppersmith, silversmith, and iron monger. The additions of brass founder, copper(smith), and iron monger are evidence of the further diversification of his talents.

The andiron is the object of particular interest in this survey of Bailey's trades and products. It appears to be about twenty-four inches tall with a tapering column mounted on a square base supported by cabriole legs with ball-and-claw feet. On the top is mounted a Federally styled vase. This engraving of an andiron made at that time is virtually

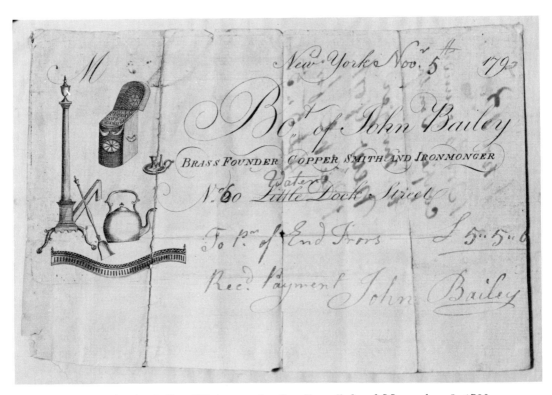

Billhead of John Bailey "To one pair of andirons" dated November 5, 1790.
Courtesy Henry Francis DuPont Winterthur Museum

absolute proof that andirons of that period were hybrids of the earlier Chippendale period (cabriole legs and ball-and-claw feet) combined with a Federal vase. A great many andirons of this style have been found; however, none of Bailey's products of that era have been located. Presumably, they were signed for it is known from later signed examples that Bailey did imprint his name on some of his products, although it is difficult to say exactly when he started the practice. The serpentine shaped fender is also evidence of the prevalence of that style at that time, and the finial on the fireplace shovel is an urn similar to the urn or vase on the andiron. The styling of these products of the brass founding trade as well as their wide variety verify the previous stated claim that Bailey was a very talented craftsman.

Sometime in the early 1790's Bailey became engaged in or associated with still another pursuit—bell founding. The following advertisement appeared in a New York newspaper:

BAILEY & HEDDERLY
NEW YORK
BELL FOUNDERY

Geo. Hedderly, from England, and John Bailey, No. 20, Little Dock Street, New York, beg leave to inform the citizens of the United States, that they have established a bell foundery, in the Bowery, where they intend casting bells, or peals of Church bells, set to music, also plantation, house bells hung on the most modern construction, bell mill, and other brasses cast, stocking frames made or repaired, either with or without the twilled, ribb'd or lace machines. G. Hedderly's ancestors, having been in the bell founding, and bell hanging business, for upwards of three Centuries past, and he having made it his study from his infancy, hopes that his abilities in the art of bell casting and hanging will merit the attention of the citizens of America.

By 1793, Bailey was using his newly built foundry for another purpose, namely, the construction of a steam jack for turning spits on the hearth. The first notice on October 21, 1793, tells that his product was exhibited in the Tammany Museum. A later advertisement by Browne and Persall indicates that they were selling it. The Browne and Persall advertisement appeared in *The Daily or Evening Register* (New York), April 16, 1794.

This was a clever device powered by steam from a heavy cast container, and converted into rotary motion applied to the spit. Jacks were the subject of much experimentation in the late eighteenth century. However, Bailey's device appears to have been expensive, and it is doubtful if many were made. At least one example has survived.

Bailey seems to have been engaged in his final lone trade as a brass founder in 1798. He was listed in New York City directories, either under the name Bailey or Bayley, from 1787 as a cutler, iron monger or founder. For most of that time (until 1803–04) he appeared to be at one location, although the numbering and name of the street changed—first to 22 Little Dock Street, and finally to 60 Water Street when the name of the street was changed in 1794. The following advertisement is from the *Commercial Advertiser,* November 19, 1798:

> John Bailey, Brass Founder, No. 60 Water Street, begs leave to inform his friends and the public in general that he has now on hand at his store, an elegant and extensive assortment of Hand Irons and other articles in the Brass Foundery, of his own manufacture. He also imported by the latest arrivals an elegant assortment of the most fashionable patterns in the plated line viz. Tea and Coffee Urns, Pots, Cram Juggs, Cruet Frames, Tea and Table Candlesticks, Bread Baskets, etc., together with every other article in the Ironmongery and Hardware Line as usual.

It is about this time that most of the signed Bailey andirons which survive today were made. One of his most frequently found styles is that of the double lemon mounted on a short round pedestal, with cabriole legs, terminating in feet of balls. He also is known to have followed another style in which a large ball (called by some experts a head) with a small ball finial are mounted on a similar pedestal with cabriole legs. The workmanship on these andirons is of good quality, and some signed examples are known today. The name Bailey is imprinted on the back side of the pedestal with a stamp of block letters.

Two views of John Bailey's "Patent Jack" for turning spits before the fire.
Courtesy J. P. Remensnyder

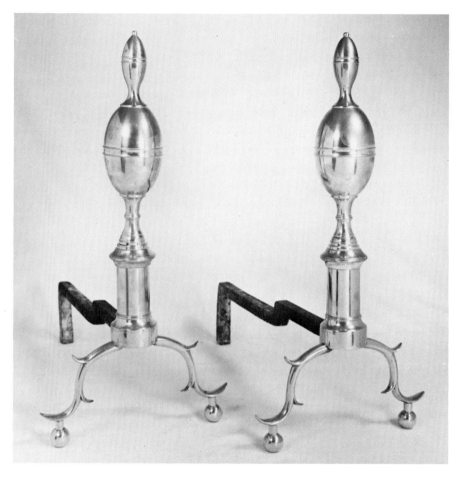

Double-lemon styled brass andirons by John Bailey of New York, ca. 1810. There is a marked similarity between the products of Bailey and Whittingham. Fortunately both men marked many of their products.
Bowers Collection

In conclusion, it must be repeated that Bailey was a very versatile workman. Judging from the press notices and the surviving examples, he was engaged in a number of trades, all oriented toward metal. He seems to have been very proficient in all of them. *Very* few historians recognize his name, but he must be regarded as one of the unsung and unnoticed men whose skills helped to bring technological distinction to the United States of America.

THE WHITTINGHAMS

It is a curious coincidence that little is known about the men who produced the greatest number of signed andirons. The Richard Whittinghams, Sr. and Jr., jointly are known to have signed more andirons than all the rest of the makers who worked in New York City late in the eighteenth and early nineteenth centuries put together. It can be safely estimated that at least fifty pair of andirons are extant which these men have made.

The crucial members of the Whittingham family are the Richards, father and son. The father was born in Birmingham, England. At the age of 43, he emigrated to America, landing in Philadelphia in 1791. He was soon given an attractive opportunity to join a society of workmen located in northern New Jersey, where a future industrial complex was planned and nurtured by Alexander Hamilton, then Secretary of the Treasury. The project at the Passaic Falls site, however, did not prove to be successful, and by 1795, Richard (Sr.) Whittingham was listed in a New York City directory as a brass founder on Henry Street. He continued to be listed in the directories until 1821. However, the last three years were probably retirement years for no trade was mentioned for him. He died on September 13, 1821, and Ann, the widow of Richard Whittingham, appeared in the 1822 directory.

Richard Whittingham had four sons, the most important one for this survey being Richard, Jr. In 1805, he was listed as a brass founder in the Jones' New York Directory. Richard, Jr., was doubtless in the business of brass founding on his own. He was listed as Richard, Jr., in the directories through 1828, but in 1829 the Jr. was dropped. He continued to be listed as a brass founder through 1841, but in 1843 and 1845 he was listed only as a founder, the implication being that either he was so well known that the prefix could be deleted, or that possibly he began casting other metals. His name does not appear in the 1850 directory, and it seems safe to assume that the omission was caused by his death.

> New York April 10 1813
>
> Mr Bird
>
> Sir Having been much engaged in some very perplexing business since you were in N York I have to regret not writing to you sooner — I now take the opportunity of informing you that I can have the order which you left (that is to say 20 pr Andirons & 20 pr Shovel & Tongs) executed in about 3 weeks if this will answer your purpose you will be pleased to write me in return
>
> Your obedient servant
> Rich Whittingham

Letter in Richard Whittingham's handwriting to Charles Bird of Bird & Co., hardware merchants located at 170 High Street, Philadelphia. The contents suggest a sizeable order of fireplace furnishings.

Isaac Whittingham was another of Richard's children who came to America with him. He also was a brass founder in New York City. His firm was located at a number of locations through 1814, but there were no separate directory entries for him until 1830. It is assumed by Henry Parrot Bascot, in his unpublished thesis *Brass Founding in New York City 1786–1840*, that Isaac worked for Richard, Sr., and Richard, Jr., during those years. In 1830, he was again operating an independent shop, and was also listed in 1831. No andirons are known that can be assigned to this maker.

Joseph Whittingham was still another of Richard's sons who was a brass founder. His business entries appear in New York City Direc-

A low-styled pair of andirons with a square pedestal marked "R. Wittingham, N/York," ca. 1795. Andirons similar to these were made by other craftsmen in the late eighteenth century.

Bowers Collection

Left and right brass andirons marked "R. Wittingham N/York," ca. 1800. Examples of left and right andirons are much rarer than those with straight billet bars.

Bowers Collection

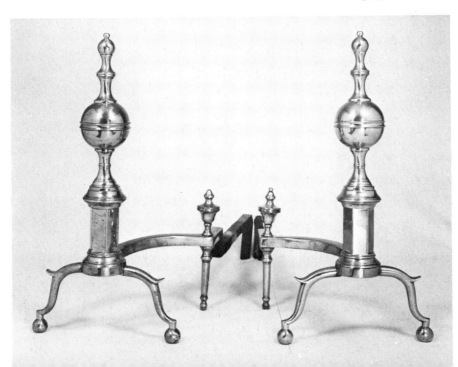

Mark of three lines on the baseplate of andirons marked "R. Wittingham, N/York." The function of these lines is not precisely known. There is a possibility that it indicated a part for andirons twenty-two inches high, as a similar mark of two lines is found on andirons of the maker which are twenty inches high.

Bowers Collection

tories from 1822 through 1850, and in 1860 he is listed as only a founder. No andirons are extant which can be assigned to this man as the maker.

It would be expected that andirons in a variety of styles came out of the Whittingham shops (father and son). Certainly one of the earliest was a tall plain cylindrical shaft, mounted on a square pedestal and cabriole legs, with either a ball-and-claw foot or a pad foot. Some of these andirons have a country scene engraved on the face of the pedestal and paterae on the sides. The column is topped with a well-designed classical vase. This pattern is obviously a final example of the Chippendale era, which seems to fit chronologically into the middle of the last decade of the eighteenth century. The Whittingham product is very similar to the example illustrated on the letterhead of John Bailey, dated 1790. The lives of these two men overlapped, and it is not surprising to find similarities in their products. This style is the scarcest of the various Whittingham products, and the name appears on the back of the plinth.

Another pattern which the Whittinghams shared with Bailey are the ones with a spool-like finial, and there are also some steeple and double lemon tops. Some comment should be made about these, for they represent a new style on the andiron scene. Their most important feature is the fact that the shaft has been eliminated, and the pedestal and head enlarged. The pedestals are either round, square or hexagonal. The examples with a square pedestal are mounted on legs joined with a square plate, with an escalloped valance on the front. Those with round and hexagonal pedestals have legs joined with a round plate which is not visible when the andirons are assembled.

It should be noted that the andirons without a shaft also have a new style of legs. The preceding examples with classical shafts have cabriole legs and feet bearing a marked resemblance to similar parts on furniture, and usually have spurs. The new legs are more slender, have spurs on the inside and outside, and are supported by feet shaped like small round balls. Sometimes the balls are attached directly to the legs, and at other times a small round rod is used as a joining device. The ratio of the size of the ball to the leg is usually quite good, but the concept is an obvious deterioration in style. Examples similar to this latter style were also made by J. Davis and J. Molineux, both of whom were located in Boston, and were working at the same time as the Whittinghams.

It is quite difficult to attribute the Whittingham products to either the father or the son. They were both working at the same time, and possibly interchanged patterns for castings because they were costly to produce. It is the opinion of many connoisseurs that at least all the signed ones were made by the father, and of course, some of the unsigned ones as well. A man in business as long as the father would have made many more andirons than the signed ones which exist today. It should also be considered a possibility that he made other products at his brass foundry, and the fact that he signed some of his products raises the possibility that other signed products of the Whittinghams will some day be found. It would not be surprising to the writers if brass candlesticks were found which could be identified as Whittingham products. As a matter of fact, it is hoped that this survey of fireplace furnishings will bring to light many new discoveries along this line.

Finally, it must be recognized that the Whittinghams were superb craftsmen. The color of their metal was good, the castings sound, and the fitting of parts was done with marked exactness. The fact that parts are interchangeable attests to the accuracy of their work. It should also be noted that they were working in the morning era of the industrial revolution in America. Their work combines the best workmanship of the eighteenth century with the exactness of the nineteenth century. They were contemporaries of Whitney who was one of the first American craftsmen to utilize the concept of interchangeable parts.

We don't know if the Whittinghams were tall or short, rich or poor, but they were not surpassed in their time in either the style or the quality of their workmanship.

CHAPTER VIII

Other Fireplace Accessories

(The definitions used in this chapter were taken from *The Oxford Universal Dictionary*, Oxford, England, The Clarendon Press, 1955.)

BELLOWS

Bellow: An instrument or machine constructed to furnish a strong blast of air. In its simplest form, it consists of an upper and lower board joined by flexible leather sides, enclosing a cavity, and furnished with a valve opening inwards, through which air enters filling and expanding the cavity, and with a nozzle, through which the air is forced out when the machine is compressed; used to blow a fire, to supply air to organs, etc.; often with reference to the two halves or handles, called a pair of bellows, rarely as singular, a bellow.

The form and function of bellows was completely established as early as the sixteenth century; since then they have undergone little change. The earliest types were up to twenty-four inches long, and were not decorated. In the eighteenth century, some were carved, while others were overlaid with decorated sheets of metal (usually brass). In the nineteenth century, many were painted, and a parlor type was decorated with arrangements of leaves and flowers. On some of the latter tv

Rotary bellows, probably of the eighteenth century.

Courtesy Ball and Ball

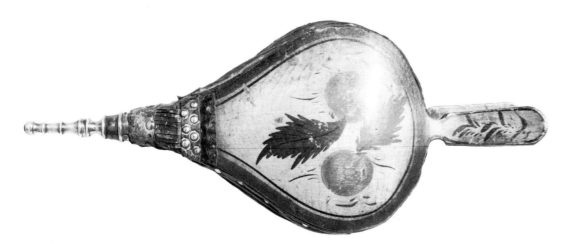

Small decorated bellows made for use at a parlor fireplace in the nineteenth century.

Kauffman Collection

the name of an American manufacturer is stamped on the flap of leather attached to the inner side of the lower board.

A comparable machine known as a centrifugal hand blower was used in England in the eighteenth century. A blowing mechanism was enclosed in a box of wood or metal, which was fitted with a handle for turning and a spout for directing the air into the fire. Their scarcity here suggests that very few of these mechanical devices were used in America.

Bellows were of such sufficient importance in 1741 that Joseph Clough advertised them as one of his major products in *The Boston Gazette*, December 15, 1741:

> Bellows Maker.—Joseph Clough near the Charleston Ferry in Boston, Makes and Mends all sorts of Bellows for Furnaces, Refiners, Blacksmiths, Braziers, and Goldsmiths; and also Makes and Mends all sorts of House Bellows after the best Manner; where all Gentlemen, and others in Town and Country may be served at very reasonable Rates.

BRAZIER

Brazier: A large flat pan or tray for holding burning charcoal.

The definition of a brazier allows a great deal of latitude as far as determining the form and function of the object concerned. They have ranged in size from one used to heat a room to that of the one

The scarcity of braziers of this type suggests that very few of them were made. Probably of the eighteenth century.
Courtesy The Metropolitan Museum of Art, gift of Mrs. Robert W. deForest, 1931

illustrated, which was used on the hearth. It has a nicely shaped bowl of copper, supported by three legs of wrought iron. The wooden handle is a convenient feature, were the braziers to be moved while filled with glowing charcoal.

This object was not only one of utility, but also one of beauty. The legs are very pleasingly shaped, serving as a support for both the brazier and the pot that stood on it. Their use, possibly on a table, is suggested by the attractive curl on the bottom end of the leg.

They are much sought after by those who want to furnish a hearth with the appropriate utensils.

Broiler made of iron by a blacksmith in the traditional techniques of his craft. Eighteenth or early nineteenth century.

Courtesy Mercer Museum

BROILER

Broil: To cook (meat) by placing it on the fire, or on a gridiron over it; to grill.

It is very interesting to note that meat was prepared by broiling before the advent of modern cooking devices. Some antique examples held the meat vertically between two grills before the fire. They were reasonably small, and when one side of the meat was done, they could easily be turned around, exposing the second side to the fire. The iron grills were mounted upright on iron legs about six to eight inches tall, so that a drip pan could be conveniently placed underneath the meat to catch the dripping fats and fluids. The rarity of these objects today suggests that they were never widely used.

Another type of broiler consisted of an iron frame, held vertically on a three-legged tripod, with hooks on which small game was attached for broiling.

Both types were made by wrought iron by the blacksmiths who worked in towns and cities along the seacoast.

CAMP STOVE

Stove: A closed box or vessel of earthenware, porcelain, or (now more usual) of metal, portable or fixed, to contain burning fuel: often with defining word, as cooking, electric, gas.

The function of these petite objects seems to be a bit hypothetical for they presumably were used for cooking, yet in the eighteenth century stoves were conceived as principally for heating. Of course, there is no proof that they are of the eighteenth century, but their style and construction suggest such a period.

The common assumption is that they were more or less a personal

Camp stove made of wrought iron and sheet iron with a turned handle of wood.

Courtesy Mercer Museum

piece of equipment, used to grill a small piece of meat over a charcoal fire or heat a small quantity of water for making coffee or tea. Regardless of their use around a campfire or on a hearth, they are very attractive objects and appropriate for the setting suggested.

CALDRON

Caldron: A large kettle or boiler.

Although caldrons were an important part of the British culinary family, few of the earliest type were used here. At least, extremely few, if any, of American production are known today. The earliest types have three long legs and two handles, all cast in one piece. By the sixteenth century, cast iron ones replaced the earlier and more expensive examples of bronze.

When equipped with a swinging handle, they were suspended over the fire to cook meat and vegetables, each one in a net so that the cooking period of each could be individually controlled. They were also used for baking by inverting them on the hearth, or covering them with a lid and enveloping them in the coals of the hearth fire. It seems certain that a tradition so strong in England would have caused the earliest settlers to use them here.

CANDLE BOX

Box: A case or receptacle usually having a lid.

Candle boxes, as the name implies, had a specialized use. Their association with the furnishings of the hearth arises principally from the fact that they were hung in the immediate vicinity of the fireplace, a convenient location when candles were removed from the box and lit for use. Most of them were round, tube-like objects about four to five inches in diameter, and about fifteen inches long, with a hinged lid.

Candle boxes were usually made of tin-plate, neatly fitted and soldered together at the joints. Examples from England are often japanned (coated with a semitransparent varnish), while American examples are of plain tin-plate, or of the same metal painted with flat black paint.

An attractive candle box of tin plate with "punched" designs on the lid.
Courtesy Henry Arnold

In Pennsylvania, examples are found with a punched design similar to that used on other boxes, chandeliers, coffee pots, etc.

Two tabs were attached to the back with large holes near the top to hang the boxes on nails. This arrangement provided adequate rigidity and permitted removal to refill with candles when supplies were exhausted.

They are a relatively scarce commodity on the antique market today, and are priced in relation to their scarcity.

CHESTNUT ROASTER

Roast: To make (flesh or other food) ready for eating by prolonged exposure to heat or before a fire.

Although chestnut roasters resemble bed warmers, the function of the two is not interchangeable. The following excerpt is from *Iron and Brass Implements of the English House* by J. Seymour Lindsay:

> Chestnut roasters of the eighteenth century and later were made of a sheet iron cylindrical box about seven inches wide by three inches deep; having the lid and sides perforated. Attached to the side is a wrought iron handle, two feet long with a wood handpiece to enable the box to be opened without burning or soiling the hands. It has a second handle attached to the lid, which when shut, lies upon and fastens to the longer handle, to which it is made fast by an iron button about half-way down the stem.

In America, examples of sheet iron are rarely found, most of them being of sheet brass. To the writers' knowledge, none have been identified as the product of an American craftsman. However, they were widely used and very decorative, and it is entirely possible that some examples were made here. If so, the name of the craftsman would probably have been placed on the top of the lid or the handle. The presence of a name does not imply that the object was made here, but it does add to the possibility that the craftsman could be identified, and that he was an American.

COAL HOD

Hod: A receptacle for carrying or holding coal.

Various refined objects were made to use on the hearth; however, none were more sophisticated than the coal hod, or vase, so named because of its similarity to objects used to carry mortar on a construction job or a container similarly shaped to hold flowers. It never was as popular in America as in England because of the fact that coal was more widely used in fireplaces abroad than here. Most of the shapes could be equally well adapted to the storage of small pieces of wood. In England, the name Purdonium became a generic term for the containers; however, that name was usually applied to an upright rectangular shape with a slanting lid.

The body of some of these objects was the subject for considerable decoration, usually applied after the outer surface was coated with a japanned finish (semitransparent lacquer or varnish). The models of the mid-nineteenth century carried hand decorations of landscapes and animals, such as one which depicted a dog named "Friend." Floral and geometric patterns were sometimes applied by the transfer method, a technique borrowed from the potters of the eighteenth century. The most elegant featured borders of transferred gold designs.

Those with painted decorations were usually made of sheet iron or steel, while other attractive forms were made of sheet copper or brass. The brass ones were made in a horizontal cylindrical shape, slightly tilted on a round base. Within the upper surface of the hod was mounted a hand scoop to transfer the coal to the grate.

These objects were also popularly known as coal scuttles; however, *The Oxford English Dictionary* does not include this name.

COFFEE POT

Coffee: A drink made by infusion or decocting from the seeds of a shrub roasted and ground or pounded.

Although coffee pots were reasonably small objects in the eighteenth century, they were quite difficult to manufacture, the spout requiring much skill on the part of the coppersmith. All the joints had to be "hard-soldered" or riveted so the parts would not separate when overheated. One might have been apt to "burn" fingers when lifting the lid.

COFFEE ROASTER

Roast: To expose (coffee beans) to heat in order to prepare for grinding.

Old coffee roasters are cylindrical forms about six inches in diameter and twelve inches long made of sheet iron. They are fitted with a sliding door, and the interior is fitted with fins which keep the coffee beans separated as the roaster is rotated over the coals on the hearth. On one end there is a long handle, on the other a short rod which could be rested on a trivet or hearth as the object is used.

Most of the examples found today are made of machine rolled sheet iron and were probably made in the nineteenth century.

CRANE

Crane: An upright (vertical) axle with a horizontal arm fixed by a fireplace, for suspending a kettle.

Cranes were always made of iron and consisted of three basic parts: a vertical bar installed in two loops projecting from the masonry of

Left, "period" coffee pots are in very short supply today. No marked examples are known which were made by American coppersmiths. *Courtesy Schiffer Antiques. Right,* the parts of a coffee roaster were obviously joined with rivets to prevent their coming apart when placed over hot coals on the hearth.

Courtesy Mercer Museum

the fireplace; a horizontal bar attached at one end to the vertical bar, which supported trammels, pot hooks, kettle tilters and pots; and a diagonal brace attached to the other two members to provide a needed support. The function of the object was to support the various utensils over the fire while food was cooking, and to swing them outward into the kitchen for removal of the food. In some large fireplaces, two cranes were installed.

They range in size from a small one, two feet long, to large examples as long as six feet. Many were made of square bars of iron which were twisted to create a spiraled decorative effect. Scrolls were sometimes a part of the diagonal bar as another mode of decoration. A very few were dated; however, they were used in America extensively throughout the eighteenth and first half of the nineteenth centuries.

Crane in the basement kitchen of the Edward Hand Plantation House near Lancaster, Pennsylvania. The twisted support arm is an attractive feature of this example.

Courtesy Edward Hand Plantation

CREEPERS

Creeper: A small iron dog (andiron) of which a pair were placed between the andirons.

Although the practice of using creepers with andirons appears to have been quite common, it is a fact that very few examples have survived. Needless to say, they were not always made of iron. The

Andirons with a matching pair of creepers. Extremely few examples are known to have survived. Of course, they may not have been very plentiful in the eighteenth century.

Courtesy Henry Francis DuPont Winterthur Museum

examples illustrated have brass columns with low arched legs and feet of iron. The use of iron for legs and feet may have been merely a matter of precedent, or it may have been due to the scarcity of brass. Or perhaps the maker considered iron to be a stronger support for the burning logs.

Traditionally, creepers were placed between the andirons to help support partially burned logs, portions of which would otherwise drop on the hearth and cut off part of the needed draft.

There is a good possibility that these were of English origin. One wrought-iron example with a trestle foot is in the Montgomery collection, and is thought to be American.

CURFEW

Curfew: A cover for a fire; a fire-plate.

The common definition of the word curfew refers to the European custom of clearing the streets with a warning that fires should be banked for the night. The fire was not put out, but was covered with a metal object in the form of a quarter sphere. The use of this object at curfew time lead to its name curfew.

Despite a reasonably wide use in the seventeenth and eighteenth centuries, they are quite scarce today. Most examples are made of copper or brass and are profusely ornamented by the repoussé technique.

DRIP PAN

Dripping: The melted fat which drips from roasting meat.

Although a drip pan was not a very attractive object, it was a necessity in every household where meat was roasted on a spit. The pan, about twelve by twenty inches and approximately two to three inches deep, was relatively simple in design, made of sheet iron or copper (those of copper being a bit more elegant). Sometimes the legs were quite short, but always high enough to keep the pan from scraping on the hearth when it was moved.

Examples are rarely found in America today. As a matter of fact, they are not common in Britain, due to the demand for them by museums with authentically furnished fireplaces.

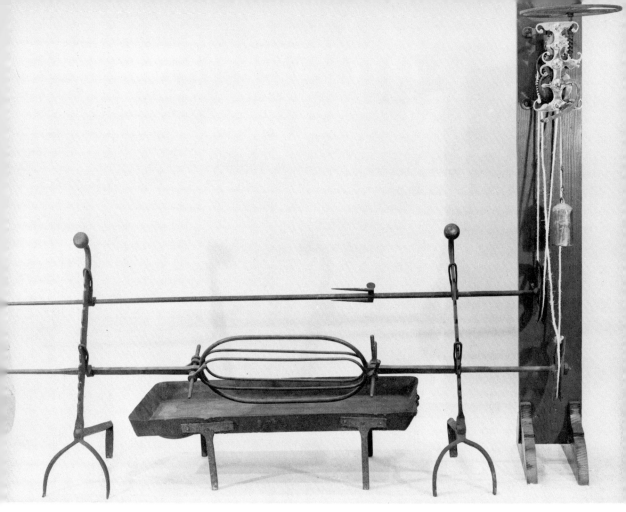

Drip pan with two styles of spits, trammel hooks on the andirons, and a clock jack usually mounted on the wall above the level of the spit. All objects are of the eighteenth century.

Courtesy Schiffer Antiques

FIREBACKS

The absence of firebricks in the back wall of the fire chamber posed at least one important problem in its operation, namely, the deterioration of the soft bricks located there. This condition was often forestalled by standing a heavy cast iron plate, called a fireback, against the back wall. There is evidence that they were used very widely in England and on a more restricted basis in America. Although examples are known to have been made in Pennsylvania and New Jersey, most

Fireback inscribed "VESUVIUS FURNACE/I. Graham." Graham operated a furnace in North Carolina in the late eighteenth century. The minimal ornamentation of this example is typical of many made in an earlier time.

Courtesy of Old Salem, N.C.

of the American firebacks have been found in Virginia and New England.

They were made by a rather primitive process known as sand-casting, on the furnace floor. First, a pattern had to be made of wood, the earliest ones having only a modicum of decoration. They were pressed into sand to the thickness of the pattern, and in early times, additional designs were pressed into the sand, in lieu of designs cut into the wood. In this process, the front and the edges of the casting were smooth and uniform; only the back side has the rough surface of cast iron. Because this area faced the back wall of the fireplace, its unfinished appearance was of no importance, and it was out of sight.

American examples are sparsely decorated in comparison to those made in England in the sixteenth and seventeenth centuries. English examples have decorations such as coats of arms, animals, and human figures of historic importance. American designers, on the other hand, used geometric patterns or folk subjects such as a cock.

Firebacks, reduced in size, later became integral parts of grates, serving the same function there as they did when standing unattached in the fireplace.

The making of firebacks was probably a brisk business in Boston in the 1740's. The following advertisement appeared in *The Boston Gazette*, July 13/ 20, 1741:

> Iron Foundry.—Any person that has occasion for Forge Hammers, Anvils, or Plates, Smiths' Anvils, Clothiers' Plates, Chimney Backs (Fire Backs), Potts, Kettles, Skillets, Cart Boxes, Chaise Boxes, Dog Irons (and Irons), or any other Cast Iron Ware, may be provided with them by Richard Clarke, at his Furnace in the Gore, giving speedy Notice (of the Sizes and Quantities they want) to him there, or to Oliver, Clarke, and Lee, at their Warehouse in King Street in Boston; where they may be supplied with Swivel Guns.

FIRE-LIGHTERS

Tinder: Any dry inflammable substance that readily takes fire from a spark and burns or smoulders; esp. that prepared from partially charred linen and from species of *Polyporus* or corkwood fungus (AGARIC L), formerly in common use to catch a spark struck from a flint with steel, as a means of kindling a fire or striking a light.

Tinder-box made of tin plate. The narrow section of the steel served as a handle to hold it when the flint was struck.

Kauffman Collection

The most common type of tinder-lighter is a low round box of sheet metal (tin-plate or brass), with a slip lid which could be removed and replaced easily. Some have candle sockets on the lid to retain a light with a candle after it was struck on the tinder with the flint and steel. Other round examples have handles which make a portable candle holder of the apparatus. One could easily be carried throughout the house whenever necessary.

Within the container, a piece of flint and steel were stored along with the tinder. In this way, all the components of the operation were held together, and only had to be replaced when either the tinder or the flint was no longer functional. The bent piece of steel lasted indefinitely.

Another form of fire-lighter was a small flint (gun) lock mounted on three legs with a container for holding the tinder replacing the pan which held the powder on a gun. These objects are avidly sought for display on a mantel shelf, a logical place for them to be placed when not in use. The flintlock type is much rarer than the round, flat tinder boxes.

FIRETOOL HOLDER

Of all the old devices remaining from fireplaces of the eighteenth and nineteenth centuries, the firetool holder is among the rarest. The scarcity of these items must relate to the fact that very few of them were made; however, it seems logical to conclude that there must have been a brisk demand for them. Their scarcity is just one of the riddles which this survey will not resolve.

FISH-KETTLE

Fish-kettle: A long, oval vessel for boiling fish.

Fish-kettles were made of light weight (thin) copper or tin plate about five-and-one-half inches deep and about twelve inches long.

This rare firetool holder is made of brass and marble. The brass part is constructed very similarly to the method for andirons, namely, the cylinder is cast in halves and then soldered together to make a tube, ca. 1820.

Courtesy Ball and Ball

Fish kettle with the names "G. and F. Harley" imprinted on the handle of the lid. The Harleys were listed as coppersmiths in the Philadelphia Business Directory for 1840.

Courtesy Mercer Museum

Their elliptical shape was designed to accommodate the whole fish. Handles were attached at the ends so they could be suspended from a trammel or a pothook. Pitched covers were fitted with a band-like handle in the center on which the maker's name was rarely imprinted. Only one is known to the writers to be the product of an American craftsman.

The insides were supplied with perforated fish plates having a handle or lug for lifting the plates out of the vessel. The entire inner surface of the copper ones and the plates were coated with tin to make it a safe vessel for preparing food, as all copper utensils should have been.

Fish-kettles were of sufficient importance for D. Crawley to mention them in his advertisement inserted in *The New York Daily Advertiser*, October 6, 1797:

> D. Crawley, Tin Plate Worker, Returns his most grateful Thanks to the public, for the very liberal encouragement he has experienced during his residence in Maiden Lane; and presuming

it might not be intruding, solicits a continuance thereof, at No. 28 Nassau Street, one door from Maiden Lane, being determined that punctuality and integrity in all his dealings shall alone evince how sensible he is of the favors conferred on him. . . .

Curious Wrought Kitchen Furniture; The Subscriber has also for sale some articles of curious wrought iron kitchen utensils, such as stew pans, sauce pans, fish-kettles, large pots, etc.

FIRE-PAN

Fire-pan: A pan for holding or carrying fire.

A fire-pan was a household necessity, particularly in the eighteenth century when fireplaces had to be lighted one from another. The pans were invariably made of sheet iron with riveted joints which were not affected by the heat of the hot coals.

The front end was shaped like a scoop so that no additional device was needed for filling. The holes in the lid provided air to keep the coals live.

Very few fire-pans are found in the market place today.

Left, fire-pan with a hinged lid and a long handle to dissipate the heat from the live coals within. *Courtesy Herbert Schiffer Antiques. Right*, a very simple example of a footman, made of brass and iron, and held together with riveted joints.

Courtesy Florence John Antiques

FOOTMAN

Footman: A stand to support a kettle, etc., before the fire.

The footman may be described as a four-legged stand of brass or iron, usually with two straight legs in the rear and two front cabriole legs. About twelve to fifteen inches high, they stood before the andirons on the hearth to hold a culinary object, such as a kettle for hot water. In many ways, they resemble a trivet, but they lack the handle and are considered less portable than a trivet.

FRYING PAN

Frying pan: A shallow pan, usually made of iron with a long handle, in which food was fried.

Frying pans have been traditionally made of cast iron, a substance whose superior properties in frying food are well known. Some of these have been marked by the makers, but by and large, they command little attention in the market place. The situation with copper frying pans is just the opposite.

Copper frying pans range from five to ten inches in diameter and two to three inches in depth. The sides are raised from a flat disc, and are planished (hammered) to make them relatively smooth. Most of the American examples have handles of cast iron attached by rivets. A few bear the name of the maker, which is stamped on the outside surface of the rim. The interior surface should be coated with tin to make its use safe for culinary purposes.

GIRDLE

Girdle: A circular plate of iron (usually cast) which is suspended over a fire upon which cakes are baked.

A girdle, or griddle, is a heavy plate of iron, usually round and supported by a handle in the form of a quarter-circle. There are also some with short legs which set on the hearth floor. They were used principally for frying pancakes, known today as griddle cakes. It is interesting to note the change in the terminology relating to this object. The word griddle does not appear in the *Oxford English Dictionary*, and the word girdle found in a modern American dictionary has a variety of meanings, none of which makes reference to a kitchen utensil. The advertisement quoted here indicates that they were called griddles in 1781.

> MOUNT HOPE FURNACE.—To Be Sold, Wholesale and Retail; or exchanged for all sorts of Country produce, and other articles, necessary for carrying on Iron Works, by the subscriber at Mount-Hope Furnace, in Morris County. All sorts of Cast Iron Kettles, Pots, large and small Tea-Kettles, Pye-pans, large and

Left, only the city (Philadelphia) can be distinguished in the "touch-mark" of this frying pan. Probably of the nineteenth century. *Courtesy Henry Arnold. Right,* circular "girdle" with handle and three legs.
Courtesy Mercer Museum

small Skillets, small Mortars, Griddles with or without legs, Wagon, Chair and Cart boxes, close Stoves, six and ten plate Stoves, open Fire-places, commonly called Franklin Stoves, Also refined Bar Iron, nail rods, nails &c. (Poughkeepsie) *The New York Journal, and the General Advertiser*, September 24, 1781.

GRIDIRON

Gridiron: A framework of parallel metal bars, used for broiling flesh or fish over a fire.

A low framework of wrought or cast iron, mounted on short legs, the gridiron was used on the hearth in a horizontal position to prepare food over glowing coals—really a horizontal broiler. One type of a later period had channeled grids which carried some of the fat to a main trough, and from which it could be drawn off. Reasonably late gridirons are usually square; many examples of the seventeenth and eighteenth century were round. Some of the round ones are mounted on a central axis so they can be rotated.

This example of a gridiron shows that they were not only practical but also had some decorative value. Probably European, eighteenth century.
Courtesy Ball and Ball

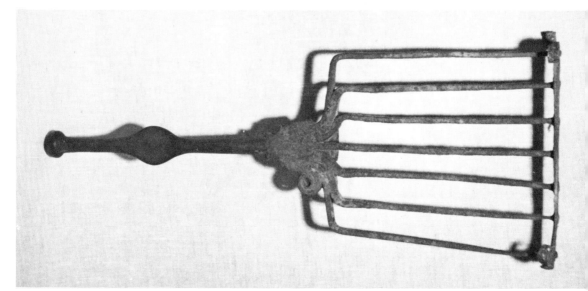

JAMB HOOK

Jamb: Each of the side posts of a doorway, window, or chimney-piece, upon which rests the lintel; a cheek; esp. in popular use (pl) the stone cheeks of a fireplace.

A small hook or open loop was attached to the jambs of a fireplace to hold tools such as shovels and tongs in an upright position. Considerable variety exists in all types, particularly those made of iron by blacksmiths, which are very rare. In the eighteenth century, very attractive ones in identical pairs were made of cast brass. A few jamb hooks have finials matching those of andirons and firetools.

Reproductions of the cast brass type have been on the market for many years, and are far more frequently found than originals. It should be noted here that it is very difficult to separate the reproductions from the originals.

KETTLES

Kettle: A vessel, commonly of metal, for boiling water, etc., now esp. a covered metal vessel with a spout.

The definition of a kettle allows the authors a wide degree of latitude in supplying specific identification. The most important American types are known as teakettles, made of both copper and cast iron, with a lone example of brass known to the authors.

The most numerous ones were made of copper in the late eighteenth and early nineteenth centuries by coppersmiths working from Massachusetts to Virginia. Very few of those made of cast iron can be identified as the products of American craftsmen, but a few are known to exist. The advantage of copper over cast iron was that they were light in weight and could be kept attractively bright by polishing,

Goose-neck copper tea kettle, signed "A. Keeney, Carlisle (PA)." A number of kettles are known which were made by this maker. Eighteenth century.

Courtesy Henry Arnold

even though they did not stay that way very long after they were put into use over the fire.

Most American examples have a spout resembling a gooseneck, without a swinging lid, the latter point usually one of the important ones in identifying an American product. Another positive identifying point was the imprinting of the name of the coppersmith on the top side of the strap handle. Many coppersmiths, particularly the early ones, had intaglio stamps for their names similar to those used by silversmiths. Sometimes these stamps have been eradicated by the constant polishing needed for the daily use of the vessel.

Although examples have been found in many parts of the eastern seaboard, most of the surviving examples were made in Pennsylvania. The workmanship is of a very high caliber, and signed examples are eagerly sought by collectors today.

Although no product is known bearing his imprint, John Halden is one of the craftsmen who advertised the making of copper teakettles. He inserted the following advertisement in *The New York Weekly Post-Boy*, November 19, 1744:

John Halden, Brasier, from London, near the Old-Slip Market in New York; Makes and Sells all sorts of Copper and Brass Kettles, Tea-Kettles, Coffee Pots, Pye Pans, Warming Pans and all Sorts of Copper and Brass Ware; He likewise mends and tins any sort of Copper and Brass, after the best Manner; at reasonable rates; and gives Ready Money for Old Copper, Brass, Pewter or Lead.

KETTLE TILTER

One of the most ingenious and, at the same time, useful appurtenances of the fireplace is the kettle tilter. It consists of three separate parts. One is a loop which is hung on a pothook or trammel; the second is the two hooks on which the kettle is suspended, and the third is a looped handle which is grasped to tilt the kettle. The con-

Cast brass jamb hooks of the eighteenth century. They were fastened to the face of the molding around the fireplace by using two screws.
Bowers Collection

Kettle tilter of wrought iron. Eighteenth or early nineteenth century.
Courtesy James A. Keillor

trivance at times has been called a "lazy back" because it permitted getting water out of a kettle without actually lifting it, and avoided the need to grasp an overheated handle. One authority states that the handle was clean, which is highly unlikely since the handle was in the midst of the fire. It was probably cleaner and less hot than the handle of the kettle which was suspended from it.

Most of the examples are not ornamented; however, their complex arrangement of parts does often make a pleasing arrangement. The writers do not know of any which have been identified as the product of an American craftsman.

LADLES

Ladle: A large spoon with a cup-shaped bowl and iron handle for ladling liquids.

Iron and brass ladles (with iron handles) were used in the rural areas of America throughout the eighteenth and nineteenth centuries. They were used at the fireplace when large quantities of food were prepared, or on special occasions such as butchering.

If surviving examples are a criterion, very many of these (with accompanying skimmers and forks) must have been made by American craftsmen. The writers have never seen any of the eighteenth century that could be identified as the product of an American craftsman, which is unfortunate, for generally speaking, they are the finest. A sizeable number have survived from the nineteenth century which were signed by the makers. Ladles of this type are sparingly ornamented, and the name may be on the back or front side of the handle. Some also have dates.

A great many have copper or brass bowls with iron handles, although some entirely of brass were made in New England bearing the name of Lee, who also worked with pewter. Some of the copper and brass bowls were made with cramped (sometimes called "dovetail") joints similar to those found in a copper teakettle. Ladles of a later period were spun on a lathe; sometimes surviving concentric marks show evidence of this technique.

Skimmer: A shallow utensil, usually perforated, employed in skimming liquids; also any utensil used for an analogous process.

Skimmers are more shallow, but often follow the same pattern as the ladles, except very few, if any, were spun.

Fork: An instrument consisting of a long straight handle, furnished at the end with two or more prongs or tines, and used for carrying, digging, lifting, or throwing; often specialized.

These culinary utensils were frequently made in sets consisting of a ladle, skimmer, and fork; sets that have not been "married" are becoming increasingly hard to find. The variant of the fork from the other two objects is simply the fact that it has tines instead of a bowl. The writers are inclined to believe that forks were at times made individually, judging from the profuse ornamentation of certain examples. Years ago, it was not uncommon to find forks with inlays of brass in the handles, often with a tulip motif.

Spatula: A simple instrument of wood, ivory, or metal, having a flat, elongated form with various modifications of shape and size, used for a variety of purposes.

On rare occasions, a spatula is found which can be mated to a ladle, skimmer and fork. These often have considerable ornamentation. Small ones are more common than large ones, some having iron handles and a blade of brass. They are sometimes part of a set which was made in Canton, Ohio, and are stamped on the back of the handle. This type is late nineteenth or early twentieth century.

The following advertisement indicates that skimmers and ladles were made as early as 1740. The advertisement appeared in *The Boston Newsletter,* October 30/ November 6, 1740:

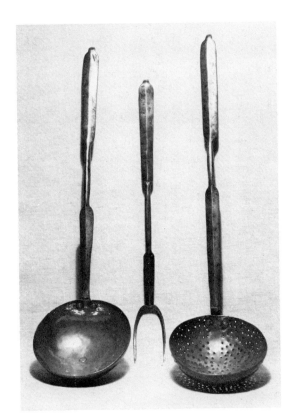 

Left, an unusually large set (twenty-four inches long) consisting of a ladle, fork and skimmer, ca. 1800. *Right,* a vertical, portable roasting oven made of sheet iron. Nineteenth century.

Courtesy Schiffer Antiques

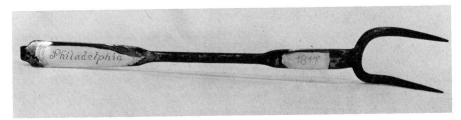

An attractive fork of wrought iron with inlays of brass on which is engraved "Philadelphia, 1817." Forks ornamented in this way are very rare.

Courtesy Mrs. Herbert Schiffer

Braziers' Shop.—Thomas Russel, Brazier, near the Draw-Bridge in Boston; Makes, Mends, and New-Tins all sorts of Braziery Ware, viz. Kettles, Skillets, Frying-Pans, Kettle-Pots, Ladles, Skimmers, Copper Pots, Copper Funnels, Brass Scales, Gun Ladles, and makes all sorts of Lead Work for Ships, Tobacco Cannisters, Ink Stands, and buys Old Brass, Copper, Lead, and Iron.

LUG-POLE

Lug: An appendage by which an object may be lifted or suspended.

Lug-poles were also called trammel-bars. Curiously, they were made of wood despite the fact that they were directly exposed to the fire in the throat of a chimney. An excerpt from *Domestic Life in New England in the Seventeenth Century* by George Francis Dow explains:

> The principle feature of this common room was its huge fireplace in which hung pots and kettles suspended by means of pot chains and trammels from hardwood trammel-bars or lug-poles that rested on wooden cross bars and so bisected the wide flue in the chimney....
> The trammel-bar in the flue also caught fire not infrequently and gave way, allowing the pots and kettles to fall to the hearth, bringing disaster to the dinner or to the curdling milk and sometimes to those seated near.

This apparatus was later changed to bars of metal, some of which remain in fireplaces today. The writers have never seen the remains of wooden bars in a chimney.

OVEN

Oven: A chamber or receptacle of brick, stonework, or iron (tin) for baking bread, and cooking food, by continuous heat radiated from the walls, roof, or floor.

Portable ovens were made of two different metals in the eighteenth and nineteenth centuries. One type was a low pot-like round casting standing on short legs. It had a lid that fitted neatly on the top and was recessed for an inch or two. The *modus operandi* of these was to place the goods to be baked within, cover with the lid, and then rake hot coals around and on the top of it until the baking was completed. Although considerable time was required to heat these devices, they stayed hot a long time after the heat of the fire receded. These are found principally in the Hudson Valley area where they were used by the Dutch, hence the name Dutch oven. This object seems to be peculiarly American for it is not illustrated in European books about kitchen fittings.

A second type of oven had the shape of a half-cylinder, with the flat, open part facing the fire, and was mounted on short legs. These were generally made of tin-plate or sheet iron. A spit was projected from one end to the other through holes provided for it, usually with a handle for manual turning. Some examples have a sliding door which could be opened to observe the progress of the roasting meat. Some also have a spout on the bottom edge to pour drippings in a container.

Another type of tin oven was also a half-cylinder, but it stood upright before the fire. A mechanized rotating spit was hung from the top, onto which the meat was attached. The spit, or mechanical jack as it was sometimes called, could be wound with a key, after which it rotated back and forward until the roast was finished.

The portable oven was an important fireplace accessory; however, of the two or three most notable accessories the built-in masonry oven must be regarded as one of the most important. We are speaking of ovens that were located in the cooking fireplace of the kitchen. They may be found in the living room of today, for in many restorations the old kitchen has been turned into the living room of the house. This transition occurred particularly in New England where houses had a small parlor in the front of the house and a large kitchen at the rear. Furthermore, primitive-like settings are very fashionable today, so the colonial kitchen is turned into a modern living room.

It is doubtful if any of the early chimneys of wattle and daub had ovens. The basis for this conclusion lies in the fact that considerable masonry work was required to build an oven, and there certainly was a minimum of masonry in such chimneys. Later, in New England, ovens were built within the masonry work of the chimney stack, this procedure being possible because of the use of many flues and the large size of chimney stacks. The earliest examples were built into the back wall of the fireplace, about thirty-six inches above the level of the hearth. They were usually built of bricks, even though the stack was of stone. That is, the roof and walls were built of brick, and sometimes a large, flat stone was used for the hearth. The earliest examples do not have a flue leading into the chimney stack, thus the live coals smouldered within the oven until it was hot enough to bake the food to be placed within. One evidence of sufficient heat was the fact that the carbon was burned off the inside walls of the oven. Ovens were almost always overheated, for it was easy to let an overheated oven cool a bit, but it was cumbersome to replace the embers, if they were removed before the oven was up-to-heat. When the oven was adequately heated, the burning embers were raked out and dropped on the hearth below. Presumably they were not totally burned; so a frugal housewife might have made further use of them on the hearth.

The roofs of many ovens were domed, and curiously, this form often remains after other parts of the oven have deteriorated. The domes were as wide as two-and-a-half to three feet, most of them being round or elliptical. Such depth required that goods be placed on a flat shovel-like instrument called a peel. This tool could reach the farthest regions of the oven and was naturally used for the removal of the baked goods as well.

At a later date, possibly early in the eighteenth century, ovens were built at the side of the fireplace, and separate from it, except that they now had a flue leading out of the oven to a chimney flue. This change was a critical one, for now fires to heat the oven burned longer and hotter. In addition, the front was closed off with a hinged door, which was most useful in the baking process. The change of location for the oven meant that the hearth had to be extended in width, in order that there would be a masonry hearth under the oven opening. The cavity under many ovens is believed to have been a place for storing wood, and is not an ash pit, as it might appear to an uninformed observer.

Masonry oven constructed on the back wall of a building in the Ephrata Cloister, Ephrata, Pennsylvania. Access to the oven was through the back wall of the fireplace within the building.

The rules for operating an oven were the same in Pennsylvania as in New England; however, many of the ovens in Pennsylvania, and regions where Pennsylvanians migrated, are built with their main portion outside the house and chimney stack. Some of these have smoke vents extending from the bottom of the back, up over the top and into a chimney flue. These are called "squirrel tail" examples.

Of course, the food had to be ready to be baked when the oven was hot. This meant that food such as bread had to be prepared the night before. Items which took the least amount of time to bake were placed in the front section of the oven, so they could be easily removed with little loss of heat, and without disturbing the food in the back. In addition to beans and bread, pies, cakes, and meat were baked in ovens of this type.

PEEL

Peel: A baker's shovel for thrusting loaves, pies, etc., into the oven and withdrawing it.

The lengths of peels vary according to the depth of the oven in which they were used. The flat end really looks like the flat end of a large spatula. They were made of wood or iron. Very few were ornamented.

POT

Pot: A vessel of rounded form, and rather deep and broad, made of earthen ware or metal (less commonly of glass) used to hold liquids or solids for various purposes.

Although the words pot and kettle seem to be used interchangeably today, it is evident to a connoisseur of culinary vessels that there is a difference. Some pots must have been used for cooking over a fire, hence the term pothook. Unlike the kettle, they did not necessarily have lids. This difference seems to be the major one between the two vessels.

A pot hook used to suspend culinary vessels at different heights over a fire.

Courtesy Mercer Museum

Pot of cast iron with three short legs for use on a trammel or on the hearth. The mechanics for casting a pot of this type were very complex in comparison to most metal castings.

Peels were made of both wood and metal, the metal ones being made primarily of iron. Handles of iron ones are frequently ornamented like the first one below.

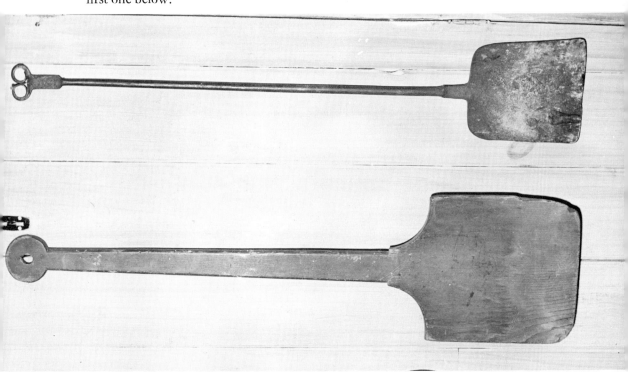

POTHOOK

A pothook and a trammel served the same function, the trammel being a bit more decorative than the pothook. There were two major parts to a pothook. One was a long strip of metal in which holes were bored at regular intervals. The other was a round bar fitted to the plate with a hook which could be inserted in any hole desired. In this way, the total length of the device could be varied to suit the needs of the moment.

The pothook, like the trammel, was hung from a lug bar or a crane in a fireplace. The second end of the bar terminated in a hook from which a kettle was hung. Thus, the major function of the pothook was to vary the height of the kettle from the fire.

PIPE RACK

Pipe rack: A rack for tobacco pipes.

A pipe rack was a device consisting of three rings of iron about four inches in diameter, connected by two horizontal bars, to which were attached two bowed legs and a ring handle. Their function is explained by Lindsay in *The Iron and Brass Implements of the English House* as follows:

> When pipes became foul with tobacco juice they were not thrown away, but were laid, as many as two or three dozen at a time, in a rack and then placed in a very hot oven until thoroughly baked, when they would be taken out quite clean and more agreeable to smoke than a new pipe. The baking did not always take place at home, but sometimes at the bakers, who made it a business to collect pipes. This was still being done about the middle of the nineteenth century at the village of Holmwood, near Dorking, in Surrey.

Pipe rack of wrought iron, with three rings and two loops for lifting. Some have only one loop in the middle which seems to be a more practical arrangement.

Courtesy Schiffer Museum

Presumably the pipe rack served a similar purpose on the hearth of the man who smoked the pipes. There is no evidence that this procedure was a traditional one in America. However, since tobacco pipes were used here, and there were also pipe racks, presumably the practice was followed here. Of course, it is possible that the racks were imported at a rather late date, but as part of the furnishings of the hearth, their use should be explained.

PIPE TONGS

Tongs: An implement consisting of two limbs or legs connected by a hinge, a pivot, or a spring, by means of which their lower ends

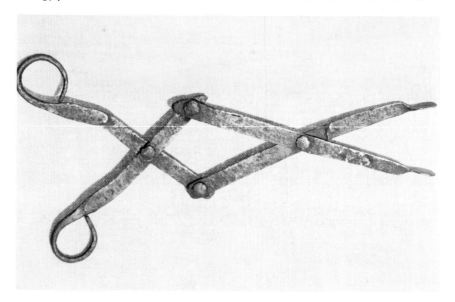

Primitive example of pipe tongs used for lifting live coals from the fire to light a smoke pipe.

Kauffman Collection

Posnet dated 1794. The names "Gay and Hunneman" are cast into the top of the handle. Hunneman and Gay formed a partnership in the mid 1790's but in 1797, they separated, when Hunneman is known to have pursued a business career of his own.

Bowers Collection

are brought together (or separated), so as to grasp and take up objects which it is impossible or inconvenient to lift with hands.

It is thought that these petite and attractive articles first appeared in the seventeenth century, soon after tobacco was first brought from America to England. They vary in length, but some are about eighteen inches long and were used to lift an ember from the hearth to light one's pipe. The jaws are sometimes kept together with a fixed spring between the handles. Many are beautifully wrought.

POSNET

Posnet: A small metal pot or vessel for boiling, having a handle and three feet.

Posnets are one of the most charming (and rare) fireplace furnishings, and fortunately some can be identified as the products of American craftsmen. They were cast of brass or bronze, with a flaring shape upward, and with the legs and handle cast as an integral whole.

The pièce de résistance is the handle on which the maker's name was cast, and sometimes his place of residence and a date. Possibly a dozen or more can be found in museums and private collections around the country today. They are considered one of the most elegant products of American craftsmen. The name on the handle is the major means of distinguishing American examples from imports.

Sauce pan with original handle of wood. This is a particularly graceful example. Eighteenth or early nineteenth century.

Courtesy Henry Arnold

RAKE

Rake: To draw together, collect, gather (scattered objects) with, or as with, a rake.

A rake was used by the baker or housewife to scrape the live coals from the oven onto the hearth after the oven reached the proper high temperature. Very few of these have survived.

SAUCE PAN

Sauce Pan: A vessel of metal, with a handle projecting from the side, and usually with a lid; employed for boiling things in cookery.

OTHER FIREPLACE ACCESSORIES 177

Sauce pans for use at the fireplace were made of several different metals, principally iron and copper, but the copper ones are understandably the most attractive. Although they were one of the standard products of the coppersmith in the eighteenth and nineteenth centuries, very few have survived until today. One possible explanation of their scarcity is that they were "worn out" and discarded. Although examples are rare, those with the names of American craftsmen imprinted on them are rarer still. The name is usually stamped on the lid, thus if the lid is lost, positive identity of the maker is virtually impossible.

SKEWER

Skewer: To fasten (meat etc.) with a skewer or skewers. A long wooden or metal pin to fasten meat or the like together, to keep it in form while being cooked (or roasted).

Skewer holder and skewers of wrought iron. Eighteenth century.
Courtesy Mrs. Herbert Schiffer

One of the most sought-after objects of wrought iron in America today is a set of skewers on a holder. The holder is usually a vertical blade of metal terminating in a loop at the top which was used to support the object by a nail. The bottom end was split, forged round (or nearly) and then spread at a right angle to the main blade, with a curl upward at the end to keep the skewers from dropping off. Their appeal lies in their charm and scarcity today. When fireplaces gave way to stoves and they were no longer needed, skewers and their holders were probably discarded. The skewer is a long nail-like object with a loop at one end to prevent its disappearing within the meat. The other end was sharpened to facilitate piercing the raw meat.

Rare skillet of copper with legs of iron. The quality of the craftsmanship suggests production in America. A piece of wood was fitted into the end of the iron handle.

Bowers Collection

Skillet of wrought iron with the name "Ibach" stamped on the handle. This is very common form, but extremely few are signed. Early nineteenth century.

Courtesy Henry Arnold

SKILLET

Skillet: A cooking utensil of brass, copper, or other metal, usually having three or four feet and a long handle, used for boiling liquids, stewing meat, etc., a saucepan, stewpan.

Posnets and skillets are remarkably similar; however, skillets seem to be of more recent vintage. They are much lighter in weight, although the handle and feet are attached to a heavier bowl. They are more plentiful than posnets; even so, examples with names imprinted on the handle are quite rare. There is no sure way to distinguish European products from American ones except the rare chance that a maker can be identified as an American craftsman. For some people, the degree of sophistication gives evidence to where it was made, the American examples being more provincial than their European counterparts. That is, edges are more precisely fitted, filed, and smoothed, and overall it is a more polished product.

SPIT

Spit: A slender sharp-pointed rod of metal or wood, used for thrusting into or through meat to be roasted at a fire; a broach.

A spit was obviously a very simple pointed rod which was thrust through a joint of meat for roasting before the fire. There is a legend that some were made of silver because they were brought to the table and used as a serving device. Most spits have a flat section near the middle through which skewers were placed to prevent the meat from slipping on the spit. There were also basket spits which had an enclosure of bars of metal attached near the center, so that the meat would be totally enclosed, but exposed to the heat from the hearth fire. Very few old spits have survived.

Bird spit made of wrought iron. The frame could obviously be raised or lowered as necessary for it to function properly. The spikes were for mounting small birds.

Courtesy Schiffer Antiques

Spit rack located over the fireplace in the Brush Everad House in Williamsburg, Virginia. Also a lavish display of other culinary tools used with a fireplace. A clock jack is located on the left side of the spit rack.

Courtesy Colonial Williamsburg

Spit Stand

Spit stands were apparently not widely used in America for extremely few have survived. They were apparently used when a spit was needed for the preparation of food but the andirons at hand did not have spit hooks.

Spit Rack

There were naturally times when a long spit was not needed, and they were a nuisance if kept lodged in the andirons. A rack of iron or

OTHER FIREPLACE ACCESSORIES 183

wood was placed on the wall above or alongside the fireplace to store the unneeded or extra rods. These are also very scarce, as they had no alternate use and would have been discarded a long time ago, together with the spit stands.

Spit stand of wrought iron with ring for handling when the stand was hot. Probably eighteenth century.

Courtesy Mercer Museum

Wrought iron toaster of the eighteenth century. Less ornamented ones, using the same rotary principle, were used in the nineteenth century.

Courtesy Gertrude Weber

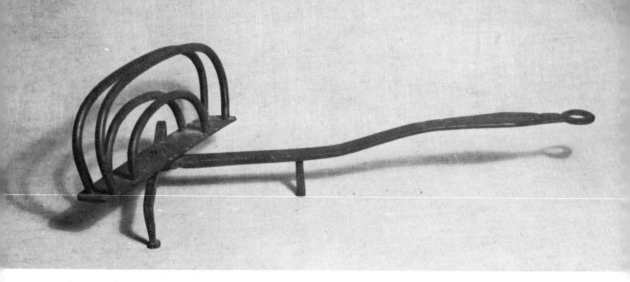

A toaster of the nineteenth century with the names "Meade and Haven" imprinted on the top side of the handle. In Longworth's Business Directory of New York City 1831–32, Haven's name is listed as a whitesmith and Meade as a blacksmith.

TOASTER

Toast: To brown (bread, cheese, etc.) by exposure to the heat of the fire.

Although a toaster might sound like a luxury item in the eighteenth century, the great number of surviving examples suggest that they must have been plentiful. Most of them consist of a handle attached to a bar, or plate, at right angle, the entire entity mounted on three legs. On top of the plate was mounted two sets of rods, half circular in form, and often twisted for decorative purposes. The plate can be rotated to brown the toast on both sides.

In the eighteenth century, toasters were made of wrought stock by a blacksmith, and ornamented in the typical way of the craft. In the nineteenth century, they were made of machine fabricated stock, and were much less attractive than their earlier counterparts.

OTHER FIREPLACE ACCESSORIES 185

TRAMMEL

Trammel: A series of links or rings, or other device. To bear a crook at different heights over the fire.

Although this definition seems to fit the description of both a pothook and a trammel, the fact is that, despite their difference in construction, their function was the same. A trammel consists of a long, thin strip of metal with a saw-toothed edge on one side in which a sliding loop fits. An iron rod is attached to the loop, and the level of the loop is determined by its position on the saw-toothed edge of the plate.

Left, trammels varied in size and decor. The large plate with the saw teeth is sixteen inches long; the shorter one is six. Neither example is ornamented. *Kauffman Collection. Right,* trivet of wrought iron with a hole in the handle for hanging when not in use. "Newton" is stamped on the handle which is a town near its present location at Doylestown, Pennsylvania.

Courtesy Mercer Museum

Another major difference between the two lies in the manner in which they are decorated. The pothook has a minimum of decoration, if any, while some trammels have a great deal. The reason for the disparity lies in the fact that the pothook, unlike the trammel, does not have much unencumbered surface to decorate. On the other hand, the broad, flat surface of the trammel invited many chased designs. The designs included birds, animals, geometric patterns, names and dates. It is very difficult to distinguish European from American examples.

TRIVET

Trivet: A stand for a pot or kettle, or other vessel placed over a fire for cooking or heating something; orig. and properly standing on three legs; now often with projections by which it may be secured on the top bar of a grate.

Most old trivets were three-legged objects of wrought iron on which utensils were supported over a bed of live coals on the hearth. It is unlikely that many of the seventeenth century have survived in America, although a sizeable number of the eighteenth century can be found in museums and private collections. Most of them were made by blacksmiths, who sometimes lavished the finest workmanship possible on them. Many are round; others are triangular, while some have fanciful shapes such as hearts, stars, and the like. Some have long handles with a loop for hanging, while others are fitted with handles of wood.

WAFER IRON

Wafer: A very light thin crisp cake, baked between wafer irons; formerly often eaten with wine, now chiefly with ices.

Wafer irons are two heavy plates of metal (iron), round or elliptical, and about three-eighths of an inch thick. The plates are at-

Waffle iron of cast iron with Pennsylvania motif.
Formerly in the Kauffman Collection

tached to two scissors-like handles, which permit them to be brought together or separated. The inside surfaces of some wafer irons are attractively decorated, and the designs are transferred to the wafers. A heavy batter placed between the two slabs of metal is baked until hard and brittle, making crisp wafer-like cakes.

WAFFLE IRON

Waffle: A kind of batter-cake, baked in a waffle-iron and eaten with hot butter or molasses. (Try honey sometime.)

Waffle irons, like wafer irons, are mounted on a scissors-like arrangement. The recessed plates, however, are covered with a network of small designs into which batter is placed and baked. Most of the examples are of cast iron, and many have attractive motifs cast on the inner surface which are impressed on the baking batter. Late models are equipped with a round stand which is placed over a circular opening in a modern coal stove. They are less attractively ornamented, but they make good waffles.

Bibliography

The Baltimore Advertiser and Business Circular For the Year 1850, Baltimore: Printed by George McGregor and Edward Lycett, binder, 1850.

BASCOT, HENRY. Brass Founding in New York City 1786–1840. Unpublished thesis, State University of New York, Oneonta, N.Y., 1972.

BRAND, WILLIAM FRANCIS. *Life of William Rollin Whittingham.* New York: Macmillan Co., 1886.

CHAMBERS, E. *Cyclopedia or, an Universal Dictionary of Arts and Sciences.* London: printed for W. Innys, J. and P. Knapton, D. Browne, T. Longman, R. Hett, C. Hitch, and L. Hawes, J. Hodges, J. Shuckbruck, A. Millar, J. and J. Rivington, J. Ward, M. Senex, and the executors of J. Darby, 1751.

COTTER, JOHN L. AND HUDSON, J. PAUL. *New Discoveries at Jamestown.* Washington, D.C.: National Park Service, 1956.

Dow, GEORGE FRANCIS. *The Arts and Crafts of New England, 1704–1775.* Topsfield, Mass.: The Wayside Press, 1927.

DOWNS, JOSEPH. *American Furniture Queen Anne and Chippendale Periods.* New York: Macmillan Co., 1952.

Encyclopedia or a Dictionary of Arts and Sciences, and Miscellaneous Literature. Philadelphia: Printed for Thomas Dobson, 1798.

Encyclopedia Perthensis, or a Dictionary of Knowledge. Perth, Scotland: Printed for C. Mitchell & Co., no date.

GOTTESMAN, RITA SUSSWEIN. *The Arts and Crafts in New York, 1726–1776.* New York: New-York Historical Society, 1938.

———. *The Arts and Crafts of New York, 1777–1799.* New York: New-York Historical Society, 1954.

HAMILTON, HENRY. *The English Brass and Copper Industries to 1800.* London: Longmans, Green Co., 1926.

JACKSON, ALICE F. AND BETTINA. *Three Hundred Years American, The Epic of a Family.* The State Historical Society of Wisconsin, 1951.

JACKSON, JONATHAN. Inventory of Boston: Suffolk County Probate Court, 1746.

KAUFFMAN, HENRY J. *American Copper and Brass.* Camden, New Jersey: Thomas Nelson Inc., 1968.

———. *The American Fireplace.* Camden, New Jersey: Thomas Nelson Inc., 1972.

KELLEY, ALISON. *The Book of English Fireplaces.* Middlesex, England: Country Life Books, 1968.

KELLY, J. FREDRICK. *Early Domestic Architecture of Connecticut*. New York: Dover Publications Inc., 1963.

KERNODLE, GEORGE H. AND PITKIN, THOMAS M. Brass Founders of New York. Antiques Magazine, LXXX, No. 4 (April 1957).

LARDNER, DIONYSIUS. *The Cabinet Encyclopedia, Vol. III*. London: Longman, Reese, Orme, Brown, Green and Longman, 1833.

LAUGHLIN, LEDLIE I. *Pewter in America, Vol. I*. Boston: Houghton Mifflin Co., 1940.

LINDSAY, J. SEYMOUR. *Iron and Brass Implements of the English House*. London: Alec Tiranti, 1964.

MITCHELL, JAMES R. Marked Andirons Made Before 1840. Unpublished thesis. University of Delaware, Newark, Del., 1965.

NEVE, RICHARD. *The City and Country Purchaser, and Builder's Dictionary*. London: Printed for D. B. Browne at Temple-Bar, J. and B. Sprint at the Bell, G. Conyers at the Ring in Little Britain; and Ch. Rivington at the Bible and Crown in St. Paul's Churchyard, 1726.

PETERSON, HAROLD L. *The American Sword*. New Hope (Pa.): Robert Halter, 1954.

PIERCE, JOSEPHINE H. *Fire on the Hearth*. Springfield, Mass.: The Pond-Eckberg Co., 1951.

PRIME, ALFRED COX. *The Arts and Crafts in Philadelphia, Maryland, and South Carolina*. Topsfield, Mass.: The Walpole Society, 1932.

PUTMAN, J. PICKERING. *The Open Fireplace in All Ages*. Boston: James Osgood & Co., 1882.

SHRIMPTON, HENRY, Inventory of. Boston: Suffolk County Probate Court, 1666.

SHUFFREY, L. A. *The English Fireplace*. London: B. T. Batsford, 1912.

SMITH, R. GOODWIN. *English Domestic Metalwork*. London: F. Lewis Limited, 1937.

SWEENEY, JOHN A. H. *Winterthur Illustrated*. New York: The Chanticleer Press, 1963.

THOMPSON, BENJAMIN. *Count Rumford's Experimental Essay, Political, Economical, and Philosophical, Essay LV., on Chimney Fireplaces*. Dublin: W. Porter and J. Archer, 1796.

WAINWRIGHT, NICHOLAS. *Colonial Grandeur in Philadelphia*. Philadelphia: The Historical Society of Pennsylvania, 1964.

Index

A

Accessories, fireplace, 137
Affluence and andiron design, 43
American andiron styles, evolution of, 43
Andirons, American, 90
  in antiquity, 17
  ball and steeple style, 14
  baluster shape of, 37
  brass, 31, 37, 94, 95, 99, 100, 102, 103, 104, 105, 106, 107, 108, 111
  of brass, making, 34
  brass on, 27
  brass finials on, 27
  bronze, 33
  cast iron, 20, 22, 67, 94, 99, 101
  cast iron in, 19
  of cast iron, making, 34
  Chippendale style for, 48
  classical, 34
  column design of, 34
  craftsmen in, 61
  curved, 14
  design of, 14
  design and affluence, 43
  double-lemon style, 14
  of the eighteenth century, 33
  of the eighteenth century, making, 56
  Empire style, 63, 67
  Federal style of, 52
  without feet, 67
  feet of, 37
  finials on, 27, 62
  and fireplace size, relationship of, 58
  Georgian style of, 48
  and grates, relationship of, 77
  heads. See Andirons, finials of
  height of, 14, 59
  height changes of, 55, 61
  kitchen type, 24
  knife blade, 50, 52, 91
  legs on, 24
  log stop on, 37
  makers of brass, 69
  makers of cast iron, 70
  manufacturing methods for, 34
  materials of, 33
  of the nineteenth century, 61
  paktong, 32, 34
  penny foot on, 34
  Queen Anne style, 40, 41, 42, 94
  reproduction of antique, 58
  Revere type, 11
  rights and lefts in, 66
  seventeenth century, 17, 20
  spit hooks on, 24
  steel, 97
  style of, 33
  and style changes, 43
  style changes in feet and legs of, 63
  style evolution of American, 43
  style evolution of columns, 40
  support for, 37
  trestle foot on, 34, 97, 99
  trestle legs on, 20
  Victorian, 68
  wrought iron, 95, 105
  wrought iron in, 17
Antiquity, andirons in, 17

B

Bailey, John, 109, 122
Baking in ovens, 169
Ball and steeple style andirons, 14
Baluster shape, andiron, 37
Bar fenders, 75
Bellows, description of, 137
  rotary, 138
Bird spit, 181
Blower, centrifugal hand, 138
Bellows, types of, 137
Brass andirons, 31, 95, 99, 100, 102, 103, 104, 105, 106, 107, 108, 111
  evolution of, 37
  makers of, 69
  making, 34
Brass on andirons, use of, 27
  Chippendale andirons, 94
  fenders, 72
  finials on andirons, 24
  technology, 27
  use of, 13
Brazier, 139
Broiler, 141
Bronze andirons, 33

C

Caldron, 142

190

INDEX

Camp stove, 141
Candle box, 143
Cast iron andirons, 20, 22, 67, 94, 99, 101
   makers of, 70
   making, 34
Cast iron in andirons, use of, 19
Centrifugal hand blower, 138
Chestnut roaster, 144
Chippendale andirons, brass, 48, 94
   style, 14
Club fenders, 76
Coal and grates, 77
   hod, 145
   scuttle. *See* Coal hod.
   vase, 145
Coffee pot, 146
   roaster, 146
Column design, andiron, 34, 40
Craftsmen in andirons, 61
Crane, 146
Creepers, 148
Curfew, 150

D

Dolbeare, John, 116
Double-lemon style andirons, 14
Drip pan, 150

E

Efficiency, improvements in heating, 79, 82
Eighteenth century, andirons of the, 33, 56
   furnishing, 14
Empire style of andirons, 63, 67

F

Federal style of andirons, 52
Feet, style changes in andiron, 63
Fenders, 71
   bar, 75
   brass, 72
   club, 76
   design of, 14
   evolution of, 71
   iron, 71
   nursery, 76
   styles of, 72
   use of, 14, 71
   use of fly press in making, 72
   wire, 74
Finials, andiron, 27, 62
   brass andiron, 24
Firebacks, decoration of, 152
   function of, 151
   manufacture of, 152
Fire-lighters, 153
Fire pan, 156
Fireplace, decline of the, 15
   Franklin, 59
   furnishings, decline of, 15
   furnishings, eighteenth century, 14
   furnishings, makers of, 109
   furnishings, seventeenth century, 13
   sets, evolution of, 72
   size and andirons, relationship of, 58
   styles and Count Rumford, 59
Fireplaces, accessories for, 137
   early, 13
   efficiency of, 14
   efficiency improvements of, 79, 82
   changes in, 58
Fire tool holder, 154
Fire tools, length of, 14
Fish kettle, 154
Flaring jambs, 14
Flask casting of brass, 28
Fly press use in making fenders, 72
Foot design, andiron, 34
Footman, 157
Fork, 164
Franklin fireplace, 59
Frying pan, 157
Furniture, fireplace furnishings and, 14

G

Georgian style of andirons, 48
Griddle. *See* Girdle.
Girdle, 158
Gooseneck kettles, 161
Grates, 71, 76
   adaptation of, 80
   and andirons, relationship of, 77
   and coal, 77
   and Count Rumford, 79
   importance of, 76
   installation of, 79
   makers of, 86
   moveable, 83
   permanent, 80
   styles of, 84
   use of, 79
Gridiron, 159

H

Heads, andiron. *See* Finials.
Heating efficiency, improvements in, 79, 82
Hedderly, George, 127
Height of andirons, 14, 59
   changes in, 55, 61
Hod, coal, 145
Hook, jamb, 160
Hooks on andirons, spit, 24

I

Identification of fireplace furnishings, 11
Improvement in fireplace furnishings, 11, 13
Iron. *See also* Cast iron, Wrought iron.
   use of, 13
   fenders, 71

J

Jackson, Jonathan, 109, 115
Jackson, Mary, 119
Jamb hook, 160
Jambs, flaring, 14

K

Kettle tilter, 162
Kettles, 160
   copper tea, 160
   gooseneck, 161
King, Daniel, 44
Kitchen type andirons, 24
Knife blade andirons, 50, 52, 91

L

Ladles, description of, 163
   types of, 163
Legs, andiron, 24
   on andirons, trestle, 20
   on andirons, style changes in, 63
Log stop, andiron, 37
Lug-pole, 166

M

Makers of fireplace furnishings, 109
Mantelpieces, use of, 13
Moveable grates, 83

N

Nineteenth century andirons, 61
Nursery fenders, 76

O

Ovens, 167
   making, 168
   portable, 167
   squirrel tail, 169
   use of, 169

P

Paktong andirons, 32, 34
Pan, drip, 150
   sauce, 176
Peel, 170
Penny foot, andiron, 34
Period styles, 13
Pipe rack, 172
   tongs, 173
Posnet, 174, 175
Pot, 170
Pothook, 172

Q

Queene Anne andirons, 40, 41, 42, 94
   period, 14

R

Rack, pipe, 172
   spit, 182
Rake, 176

Reproductions, andiron, 58
Revere type andirons, 11
Roaster, chestnut, 144
   coffee, 146
Rotary bellows, 138
Rumford, Count, and fireplace styles, 59
   and grates, 79

S

Sauce pan, 176
Saugus Iron Works, 20
Scuttle, coal. *See* Coal hod.
Sets, evolution of fireplace, 72
Seventeenth century, andirons of the, 17, 20
   furnishings, 13
Shrimpton, Henry, 109, 110
Signatures on fireplace furnishings, 14
Size of fireplaces, changes in, 58
Skewer, 177
Skillet, 178, 179, 180
Skimmer, 164
Spatula, 164
Spit, 180
   bird, 181
   hooks on andirons, 24
   rack, 182
   stand, 182, 183
Steel andirons, 97
Stove, camp, 141
Style and andirons, 33, 43

T

Tea kettles, copper, 160, 161
Tilter, kettle, 162
Tinder, 153
Tinderbox, 153
Toaster, 183, 184
Tongs, pipe, 173
Trammel, 185
Trammel-bars. *See* Lug-poles.
Trestle foot, andiron, 34, 97, 99
Trestle legs, andiron, 20
Trivet, 185, 186

V

Vase, coal, 145
Victorian era, andirons of the, 68
   styles of the, 15

W

Wafer iron, 186
Waffle iron, 187
Whittingham family, 109, 131
   Isaac, 132
   Joseph, 132
   Richard, Jr., 131
   Richard, Sr., 131
William and Mary period, 14
Wire fenders, 74
Wrought iron andirons, 17, 23, 95, 105